"....The best way I can describe ol' Dan is that he represents a true to life, God fearing, rough and tough, honest, funny as hell, call a spade a spade West Texan! When God created West Texas, he created a nasty spring wind out of the southwest, abundant sand, beautiful sunsets, and Dan Fields. I hope you enjoy this collection of Dan's stories from his childhood and adult experiences as much as I have had the privilege to do so firsthand while traveling with Dan across the many farm to market roads across West Texas getting educated on the cotton industry and the many people in it that Dan so dearly cherishes."

— Lynn Scherler, Regional Vice-President, CoBank

"—Dan Fields lived what he writes about and it shows. His stories are authentic and moving. He is a gifted writer."

— Ginger Rutland, Sacramento Bee

"Yours is a powerful story, one that needs to be preserved."

— Dr. Bob Kern,
Iowa State University

"—The raw richness of Dan Fields' powerful storytelling rivals Larry McMurtry and Frank J. Dobie. It's more than Texas history; it's a delight."

— Don Fields, President,
RF Communications, Inc.

"—a remarkable bit of writing about cattle ranching in Texas during the Dust Bowl days of the Depression. I think you will agree that Mr. Fields 'walks the walk'. I think you'll find his work to be both compelling and extremely touching."

— Ed Sulzberger, Chairman, Aid to Africa

"The Day They Killed the Cows" really puts you there in the moment. Fascinating."

— Gail Pennington, Former Editor for International Center
for Tropical Agriculture, Cali, Columbi

"Dan Fields, manager of State Line Coop since 1969 was named Cooperative Ginner of the Year for 1988 by the Texas Agricultural Cooperative Council. Well known throughout the Higginbotham community for his humor, sound business judgment and involvement, Fields also is known for initiating and completing projects. According to one nomination, State Line has come further than any other gin on the Plains. They were broke and now they are one of the strongest gins we have. In my mind, no one deserves this honor more than Dan Fields.

Fields service extends beyond the gin's property lines. While president of Plains managers Association he was instrumental in forming South Plains Industrial Supply, a new cooperative that has saved gins countless dollars for equipment and machinery."

— Summer, 1997,
COMMENTATOR

"The Day They Killed the Cows is a very beautiful story—absolutely gripping, quiet and taut as a wire. May there be many more."

— Dr. Ken Fields,
Professor of English,
Stanford University

"—You are a great writer! You need to publish your stories."

— Marie K. Thompson,
Former Coordinator of the Information
and Communication Unit,
International Fertilizer Development Center
Muscle Shoals, Alabama

"Many thanks to you and Joyce for the sacrifices you have made in order for people to enjoy themselves so much at our Texas Agricultural Cotton Council conferences in Ruidoso and for all the effort you put into these meetings. You are a great fit!

— Tommy Engelky, President,
Texas Agricultural Cotton Council

The Day They Killed the Cows

The Day They Killed the Cows

&

Other Memories of a West Texas Pioneer

BY

Dan Fields

Foreword by Dr. Tom Hargrove

Happy Valley Publishing

The Day They Killed the Cows

This publication contains the opinions and ideas of its author. It is intended to provide historical information and humorous incidents and insights about the author. It is not intended to substitute for the services of qualified professionals.

Inquiries should be addressed to:

HAPPY VALLEY PUBLISHING
8609 Jordan Dr.
Lubbock, Texas 79423

www. danfieldsbook.com

FIRST EDITION

Fifth Printing 2010

Cataloging in Publication Information:

Fields, Dan

The Day They Killed the Cows and Other Memories of a West Texas Pioneer

1. Dan Fields—Biography. 2. West Texas—History—Twentieth Century. 3. Texas—Life and customs. 4. Cowboys—Texas Biography. 5. West Texas—Culberson County—Gaines County—Kent County—Mitchell County—Stonewall County—Wilbarger County. I. Author. II. Title.

F 391.2 E 365 F9 978.008 Fi 2006938847

Cover photograph of shooting the cows
courtesy of the Southwest Collection, Texas Tech University, Lubbock, Texas.

International Standard Book Number-13: 978-0-9789628-0-7
International Standard Book Number-10: 0-9789628-0-X

Printed in the United States of America
at
Morgan Printing
Austin, Texas

To Joyce,
my wife
my love
my strength
my friend

TABLE OF CONTENTS

PART III
FIFTIES PIONEERS AT HIGGINBOTHAM, TEXAS

PART IV
TRUCKING, GINNING AND SURVIVING

PART V
LAUGHING, LOVING, AND DEATH

Foreword

Dan Fields epitomizes West Texas. He's a cowboy, cotton farmer, rancher, and cotton ginner. I'm proud to be the nephew of Dan and Joyce Fields.

Dan taught me, as a kid, Texas skills and ethics that one should use throughout life. He started with how to sharpen a knife, sight-in a rifle, lead a dove, clean game—but those basics led to other ethics, like to always respect my elders, and that a handshake should be as good as any legal document a lawyer can write.

Dan is a storyteller. A good one. He should be; he's practiced all of his life. When Dan tells a story, you're there, decades ago... years ago . . .or this morning. You'll laugh at some of his stories, cry at others. Dan's stories can be heartrending and personal—or outrageous. He also tells a good joke, that can always make you laugh. But if you want only politically correct stories and jokes, stay away from Dan Fields!

Country wisdom lies beneath Dan's crusty facade. Dan is practical, far too honest, light on social skills (except when he uses them to his advantage), and a person who truly cares for other people.

The first story of this book, The Day They Killed the Cows, is gripping and haunting. Dan takes us back to when, as a boy of seven, he watched one of the saddest events of U.S. agriculture in Scurry County, Texas, during the Dust Bowl and Depression. The story reminds me of a poignant scene in Hud, Larry McMurtry's novel, then movie, where Homer Bannon, an honest and traditional West Texas rancher, had to allow government men to shoot his cattle herd, built up over decades, because some animals were infected with hoof-and-mouth disease. Dan's story was originally published in The Cattleman. A friend wrote, after reading it, "I've always imagined what it was like to grow up in rural West Texas during the Depression. Now I know. Dan Fields' story is a window to that era."

Dan's stories all share a common theme: a life of farming and ranching in West Texas. Of horses and mules. then tractors and pickups. Of going through hard times, and good times—but always with humor and a positive attitude. Texas stories.

I personally relate to many of Dan's stories because I grew up on a red dirt, dryland cotton-cattle farm in neighboring Fisher County during the Great Five-Year Drought. My father never made a cotton crop from 1951 through 1955. Local farmers and ranchers often say that we learned that jack rabbits make good chili during the Drought. We were poor, but I didn't know it...because our neighbors were far poorer. But the Hargrove family, even during the Great Drought, was rich compared with how Dan Fields grew up during the Depression.

Dan writes first about ranching and farming 20 miles from Snyder, in Scurry County, then near Colorado City, in Mitchell County. In 1952 Dan and Joyce, along with Dan's parents Julius and Fannie Fields, moved, as true pioneers, to the flat open prairie of Higginbotham Community in Gaines County, Texas. Dan and Joyce broke the land, drilled irrigation wells, planted crops, and started a new farm and ranch operation right on the New Mexico border. I remember, as a kid, plowing in Dan's cotton fields in Texas, then invading New Mexico to turn the tractor around at the western end of each row.

Dan also started State Line Trucks, hauling cotton and farm supplies. He was gin manager at Higginbotham, then was associated with cotton cooperatives for years. Dan always advocated, tirelessly, for farmers and ranchers

Dan received a special award, after several record ginning years, in 1989. It was officially called Ginner of the Year, but farmers and ginners called it the Best Damn Cotton Ginner in Texas award—the title of one of Dan's stories.

Dan sold his last cow and ginned his last bale of cotton in the early 1990s. But he was immediately recruited to establish, then be president of, South Plains Industrial Supply, a Lubbock-based supplier for cotton gins.

In 1997 the Texas Agriculture Cooperative Council officially named its annual golf competition the Dan Fields Invitational Golf Tournament, held in Ruidoso, New Mexico.

I've been an agricultural journalist all of my adult life, working mostly with the International Agricultural Research Centers in Asia, Latin America, and Africa. We developed and spread the improved varieties of rice and wheat that launched the Green Revolution in Asia and Latin American agriculture. We're now trying to launch a Green Revolution in Africa.

I consider Dan's compilation of stories a remarkable work of agricultural journalism—a history of rural Texas that has almost been lost. But Dan doesn't claim to be a journalist; he's proud to be a farmer, a rancher, a cowboy.

That cowboy and Joyce once walked with me, even though we were thousands of miles apart, on an 11-month forced march when I was held hostage in the high Andes of Colombia. Communication was impossible, but I always knew that Dan and Joyce were there… not only for me but more important, for my wife Susan.

This book is important not only for its historic content, but also because it increases the audience for Dan Fields' stories. Introducing this book—and this man—is an honor. I hope you enjoy the stories as much as I did the first…and the fortieth…time I heard them.

Tom Hargrove, Editor and Head, Communication Unit
IFDC: an International Center for Soil Fertility
and Agricultural Development
Muscle Shoals, Alabama
20 September 2006

Dr. Thomas R. Hargrove is author of Long March to Freedom: Tom Hargrove's Own Story of His Kidnapping by Colombian Narco-Guerrillas, which inspired the Warner Bros major motion picture Proof of Life. Long March is now available at www.authorhouse.com. Hargrove also wrote the books A Dragon Lives Forever: War and Rice in Vietnam's Mekong Delta (authorhouse.com); and The Mysteries of Taal: A Philippine Volcano and Lake, Her Sea Life and Lost Towns (Bookmark, Manila).

Acknowledgements

My sincere thanks to my wife Joyce and children, Danna, Debby and David, who patiently listened to these old stories over and over before a pen was ever put to paper. They still demanded that I write them.

Without the countless hours of hard work by Joyce and Danna, this book would have never been published. I could have never done this without the insistence of Gene Beck, Dick Cooper and the rest of my many friends that I put these tales on paper.

Thanks to Lea Kidd for bodily loading me up and forcing me to go to my first writing class which was taught by Nancy Kastman-Scott.

Nancy had taught writing in Kansas on both high school and college levels, before her retirement in Lubbock, Texas where she quickly and generously started several free classes. Her tireless and skillful efforts guided me through the writing of these stories and I will be forever grateful to her.

This page would not be complete without expressing my deep appreciation to two of my nephews: Don Fields and Dr. Tom Hargrove for their endless encouragement and support.

PART I

Early Years

CHAPTER 1

The Day They Killed the Cows

People who lived in the Southwestern part of the United States in 1934 had a very rough time getting by. My family and neighbors were no exception. The dry weather, which started in 1933, worsened in 1934. Drought conditions extended throughout eastern Colorado, Kansas, Oklahoma, New Mexico and Texas, an area of approximately fifty million acres. The top soil was dry and pulverized. The few rains that came, fell hard, sealing the ground over so that most of the water ran to the low places or into the creeks.

Those two years were the worst days of the "Dust Bowl."

West Texas had more than its share of sandstorms when howling winds up to seventy miles per hour wreaked havoc with the topsoil. Drifting sand piled up on fences, barns, houses and anything else that slowed the wind. The days when the dust came were completely different, a strange phenomenon. Usually, we saw a thin black line on the northern horizon which slowly drifted toward us, sometimes taking a half-day to arrive. This was black soil blown up by ferocious winds in Colorado, Western Kansas, the Oklahoma Panhandle and the North Plains of Texas.

We lived at Camp Springs, Scurry County, Texas, and found it unbelievable that there was little wind with the dust. While we worked outside, we watched carefully as the dust approached so that we were able to get home before it arrived. It drifted in like a black cloud as fine as face powder. It settled on everything. Sometimes it became so dark during the day; the chickens went to roost, and we were forced to light the old coal oil lamps which lighted our house.

We had made a little cotton and some feed in 1933, but 1934 brought almost no rain. We made no cotton and hardly any feed. The feed was Hegari, a grain sorghum which grew to a height of about five feet with a head of grain on top. We called it Hi-gear, don't ask me why. Normally the feed was cut and tied in bundles by a row binder pulled by a team of mules; then the bundles put in shocks, and when dry, hauled to the stack lot, near the barn. Bundled feed was essential to make a crop because it was what we fed our horses and mules. Some was fed to our cattle, but mostly it went to the horses and mules, as they could not do much work without it. A farmer without feed was out of luck! It was like a modern-day farmer without diesel for his tractor.

My dad knew better than anyone that we could not go into fall and winter without feed; but the Hi-gear had only grown where a little water had stood. It was not much over knee-high, too short to be tied by a binder, so Dad sawed the handles off some garden hoes, leaving them about fourteen inches long and sharpened them to an almost razor-like edge. Then he and my brothers, J.C. and Rex, cut that feed by hand with those short handled hoes. They made bundles and tied them, by hand, with twine. "Back-breaking" does not fully describe this kind of work. I was seven years old and too small to cut feed, so I carried twine and water to them.

We barely had enough fodder for our teams, and none for the cattle. Our grass was gone; so things looked awfully bleak. Many people had no feed, or weren't industrious enough to work so hard to gather the small amount they had grown.

Most of the cattle in the drought area were thin and undernourished; some were starving. The earthen tanks were dry, and some of the creeks had dried up; so most of the water was pumped by windmills, causing many people to be short of water. The majority of farmers and ranchers had disposed of a large part of their herds; but nearly everyone had some stock left. Many of these would not make it through the winter. The situation was grim.

Franklin D. Roosevelt was serving his second year as President. Both he and the Congress realized that the agrarian economy of the United

States had to be given a boost if the country was to recover from the Great Depression. They initiated a voluntary program to help farmers and ranchers in the drought stricken area. The government bought the young, strong cows and big calves and shipped them north to grass. The price was $15.00 for the cows and $8.00 for the calves. They killed the thin, weak animals. For them, the price was $12.00 for cows and $4.00 for calves. They hired hundreds of men from across the southwest, to dispose of the weaker cattle by shooting them. They worked every day of the week and hundreds of thousands of cattle were killed. Owners could either let the cattle starve or sell them to the government and get a little money. The choice was difficult, but everyone we knew sold out and paid a few bills with the money they received.

The controversial program was all people talked about for weeks. Dry weather and cows was the only topic of conversation at our house during this time. It was a strange and emotional situation. Nobody had ever seen anything like this, and thank Goodness, no one will ever see it again.

There were a lot of hungry people in the United States during that time, and some of them were folks we knew. Ideally, a program such as this would have provided food for those people; but as in all government undertakings, there was a flaw in this one—regulations prohibited using the meat, which nobody understood. The cattlemen, however, soon discovered that the government shooters were sympathetic and left before the ranchers finished burying the cattle, giving each of them the opportunity to save the meat from a calf. At first, the general public knew when and where the killings were to take place, and dozens of people came to the sites, which interfered with the work. Some of them even got into the slaughter pens and fought over the meat while the shooting took place. This had to stop; so the schedule of the government men was kept secret. Only the people who owned the cattle knew the date when their animals were to be shot. Small groups of neighbors were assigned a date and location to take their cattle, in order to expedite the slaughter—only they knew the date of the killings.

The morning came when we were to deliver our cattle, so we were up before daylight. Dad, my brothers and I saddled up our horses and drove them three miles to a neighbor's place where we met three or four others with their small herds. The first thing I did was to pick a ring-side-seat on the roof of a shed by the main corral, where I could see everything that went on. I didn't intend to miss a thing. I had heard so much talk regarding the event about to take place, that in my child's mind; it was beginning to look like a sensational and exciting adventure. When the government man came, the cattle were counted and sorted according to age and condition. After the paper work was completed, the ones to be killed were herded into the large corral, cows and calves together. The stage was set.

The government man went to his car and took out a pump action .22 caliber rifle and lots of shells. He carefully loaded his gun, smoked a cigarette, and stepped into the corral as casually as if he were going for a walk. There were a dozen people watching; but the only sound was a cow bawling for her calf. Every eye was glued on the shooter. He was standing right below me; and I jumped when he chambered a shell into the gun. He raised the rifle—a sharp crack rang out; a cow crumpled and fell on her side, legs jerking.

Government shooter killing cattle. (Photo courtesy of Southwest Collection, Texas Tech University)

Three seconds later, Bang! Another cow went

down—and another—and another—and another! Within a minute fifteen cows were dying before my eyes. I suddenly realized that I was in the wrong place. Hot water came up in my mouth, and I had an awful feeling in the pit of my stomach; but I couldn't leave; I was afraid I would be called a sissy if I let anyone know. The man slowly reloaded, let his gun cool for a minute, then the slaughter continued. Shot after shot rang out. For me, the calves were the worst part. I shut my eyes part of the time. Finally, it was over and I started to breathe again. Within fifteen minutes, out of more than a hundred animals, not a cow or calf was standing. The shooter calmly unloaded his

CO-OPERATIVE EXTENSION WORK
IN AGRICULTURE AND HOME
ECONOMICS

AGRICULTURAL AND MECHANICAL COLLEGE OF TEXAS
AND UNITED STATES DEPARTMENT OF
AGRICULTURE CO-OPERATING

STATE OF TEXAS

EXTENSION SERVICE
COUNTY AGENT WORK

Roby, Texas,

Mr. Jas. B.Day
Rotan, Texas

Dear Sir:

There is enclosed herewith check(s) for $ 35.00 in payment for the cattle which you sold to the Government under the Emergency Drought Relief Program.

If the amount is correct please sign the receipt below and return to this office, using the enclosed self addressed envelope, which requires no postage.

There is also enclosed a copy of Public Voucher and Emergency Cattle Agreement to be retained by you for your files.

Very truly yours,

Knox Parr, County Agent.

RECEIPT FOR CHECK

Cover letter of a Public Voucher for cattle killed as part of Franklin Roosevelt's Drought Relief Program.
(Courtesy of Bill Day, Rotan, Texas, son of James Day)

Form No. Cattle 2b
U.S. DEPARTMENT OF AGRICULTURE
AGRICULTURAL ADJUSTMENT ADMINISTRATION
Approved by Comptroller General U.S.
June 2, 1934

This copy to be retained by the producer

D.O. VOUCHER NO. ________
No. ________
APPROPRIATION ________

PUBLIC VOUCHER AND EMERGENCY CATTLE AGREEMENT

(Voucher prepared Roby, Texas, December 15, 1934 *)*
(City, State, and date)

The UNITED STATES, *Dr.*, TO—

Line A Jas. B. Day.
(Producer)

hereinafter referred to as the "Producer."

Line B None
(Lienholder(s) or lienholder's(s') designated payee(s))

hereinafter referred to as the designated payee and the producer jointly.

(The Producer to receive total of benefit payment specified in column 4, Table A, below; producer and lienholder(s) or lienholder's(s') designated payee(s) jointly to receive purchase payment specified in column 6, Table A, below. If there are no lienholders, total amount entered in columns 4 and 6 of Table A, will be paid to producer.)

Paid by

(For use of paying office)

Producer's post-office address ______ (R.D. No.) ______ (Box No.) Rotan, (Post office) Texas. (State)

Producer operates farm known as In Rotan, situated ______ (Miles and direction)

from ______ (Town) on ______ road, in Rotan Township, in

Fisher County, State of Texas

TABLE A

ITEM No.	CLASSIFICATION Column 1	NUMBER OF HEAD Column 2	BENEFIT PAYMENT PER HEAD Column 3	BENEFIT PAYMENT AMOUNT Column 4	PURCHASE PAYMENT PER HEAD Column 5	PURCHASE PAYMENT AMOUNT Column 6	FOR AUDIT USE ONLY
	CATTLE: Two years and over—						
1	Condemned		$	$	$	$	
2	Accepted for use	1	6	6.00	9	9.00	
3	Accepted for use	1	6	6.00	14	14.00	
4	Accepted for use						
5	Accepted for use						
6	Accepted for use						
	YEARLINGS: One to two years—						
7	Condemned						
8	Accepted for use						
9	Accepted for use						
10	Accepted for use						
	CALVES: Under one year—						
11	Condemned						
12	Accepted for use						
13							
14							
	TOTAL	2		$ 12.00		$ 23.00	

Bureau of Animal Industry Inspector's Certificate of Receipt

I CERTIFY that the cattle described in Table A, after proper classification and due inspection, have been received and accepted for and in behalf of the Secretary of Agriculture or disposed of as directed; that they were procured under the agreement herein, and that the amounts charged are just and reasonable and in accordance with the agreement.

R. J. [illegible]
Inspector, Bureau of Animal Industry.

(Do not use this space)
Differences ______ $ ______

Account verified; correct for (total columns 4 and 6) ______

Initials ______

Producer's Certificate and Signature

I hereby subscribe to the agreement printed on the reverse hereof and certify that the amounts stated in Table A are correct and just and that payment therefor has not been received.

Witness [signature] ______ (Producer's signature) [L.S.] December 15, (Date), 1934.
Witness Carl G. Mask ______ (Producer's signature) [L.S.] ______ (Date), 1934.

Lienholder's Certificate and Signature

I hereby subscribe to the agreement printed on the reverse hereof and certify that the amounts stated in column 6

Bureau of Animal Industry Inspector's Certificate of Receipt.
(Courtesy of Bill Day, Rotan, Texas, son of James Day)

EMERGENCY CATTLE AGREEMENT

Pursuant to the Agricultural Adjustment Act, approved May 12, 1933, as amended

PERFORMANCE BY PRODUCER

The producer agrees:

(1) To sell and convey the cattle described in Table A to the Secretary of Agriculture (herein referre to as the Secretary) by delivering such cattle to an agent of the Secretary authorized to accept delive thereof and by disposing of any such cattle in such manner as may be directed by an authorized a of the Secretary.

(2) To cooperate with further general programs pertaining to the adjustment or reduction of duction and/or for the support and balance of the market for cattle and/or dairy products which n be proffered by the Secretary, pursuant to the Agricultural Adjustment Act, as amended. To execut the agreements necessary to participate in such programs and necessary to share in the payments that may be paid by the Secretary for performance thereof, and the producer agrees that the total or any part thereof of the "benefit payment" for the cattle described in Table A hereof may be applied to and deducted from any payments he may become entitled to under any such agreement or agreements.

It is understood that the Secretary may require signers of Emergency Cattle Agreements to agree to special terms and conditions and to furnish special or additional information and evidence as a part of any such general program or programs.

(3) Not to sell or assign, in whole or in part, this agreement or his right to or claim for the benefit payment under this agreement, and not to execute any power of attorney to collect such payment or to order that any such payment be made. Any such sale, assignment, order, or power of attorney shall be null and void.

(4) To abide by and conform to regulations and administrative rulings relating to emergency cattle agreements (which are and shall be a part of the terms of this agreement) heretofore or hereafter prescribed by the Secretary.

(5) That he is signing this agreement in consideration of the total payments set forth in columns 4 and 6 of Table A, being made as set forth on lines A and B on the reverse hereof, and recognizes the "benefit payment" as made in consideration of his participation in the reduction of production effected by this agreement.

REPRESENTATION AND WARRANTIES

The producer represents:

(6) *a.* That he is operating the farm described herein.

b. That he has owned and has been in possession of cattle described in Table A since April 1, 1934.

c. That the subscribers hereto include all persons owning or having an interest or lien in and to the cattle described in Table A.

d. That the subscribers hereto have good right to sell such cattle free and clear of all encumbrances and that the producer will warrant and defend the same against lawful claims and demands of all persons.

AGREEMENT BY LIENHOLDERS

(7) The subscribing lienholder(s), in consideration of the Secretary's undertaking to make payment of the "purchase payment", which is set forth in column 6 of Table A, jointly to the payee(s) designated in line B, on the reverse hereof, and to the producer, and in consideration of the other agreements and undertakings of the parties hereto, hereby release(s) and forever discharge(s) from all claims and liens now or hereafter owned or held by the lienholder(s) the cattle described in Table A and agree(s) to apply to any indebtedness secured by any such lien or claim any and all amounts received by the lienholder(s) from payments under this agreement and to execute and acknowledge such documentary evidence thereof as may be requested by the other parties hereto, and hereby waive(s) any claim to the amounts set forth in column 4 of Table A which are to be paid solely to the producer hereunder and agree(s) not to bring, or have brought, suit or proceedings to have such sums applied to any claims or debt and agree(s) to permit the producer to perform this agreement.

Emergency Cattle Agreement Rules.
(Courtesy of Bill Day, Rotan, Texas, son of James Day)

rifle, got into his car, and drove off. The work for Dad and the other men was just beginning. The dead animals had to be dragged away from the corral to a deep pit, which had been dug previously by the ranchers, then covered with dirt. The work wasn't over: the carcass each rancher had saved had to be butchered.

I didn't have much to say on the way home. I was numb. The calf which Dad and my brothers had butchered was hung on the windmill tower for the night, to cool and be cut up and canned the next day. Canning in those days was putting the meat in jars and pouring hot grease over it. When it cooled, it solidified, sealing the meat. However, it became rancid if kept too long. We cut off enough fresh beef for supper that night, but it didn't taste good to me. It had been a long, sickening day. I went to bed early; but I didn't sleep well. Dreams of dying cattle kept waking me. I did not realize, at my age, that the same slaughter was taking place every day at hundreds of locations, all over the southwest. Thousands of cattle died.

This was a terrible thing for anyone to witness, especially for a seven year old child. That happened more than seventy years ago, and many times, through the years, I have shut my eyes and vivdly recalled the sound of the shots, the bawling of the cattle, the fear in the eyes of the animals, as they seemed to realize what was happening—but most of all: the shots ringing out, over and over and over.

Everyone my age can tell you where they were when they heard the Japanese had bombed Pearl Harbor. They can also tell you what they were doing when they heard that President Kennedy had been shot. I can also remember a third event, which I recall with the same clarity. I know where I was and what I was doing in 1934, the day the cattle were killed.

Chapter 2

Worm Stomping Incident

I'll bet some of you have accidentally stepped on a worm known as a caterpillar. What a mess! I was formally introduced to this pest at age 5. We called them "wooly worms."

My family farmed at Camp Springs, Texas, in 1931. We had one ten acre patch of cotton which was totally surrounded by pasture. These caterpillars, or wooly worms converged on that cotton field when it was barely out of the ground. Those worms went down the rows, eating away, clipping off the little stalks. That was before we had insecticides, and Dad was worried about losing that small cotton patch. He'd hinted that he might send me down to the field to kill the worms.

I'd forgotten about the worm conversation. One day, I sauntered off down to the field to see Rex, my older brother. He was plowing with a mule-drawn, single-row cultivator. I stopped to visit with him, and he said, "By the way, Dad said for you to stomp these worms this morning." I had some fun things in mind, so I didn't think that was a very good idea. Then he added, "I'll tell you this: you'd better get busy, because you know that Dad means what he says."

Reluctantly, I said, "All right," and started knocking worms off the plants and killing them with a stick.

Rex said, "Dad didn't say to kill those worms with a stick; he said to stomp them."

"I'm barefooted!"

"That doesn't matter; he said to stomp them."

"Having learned to cuss at a tender age, I yelled, "Well, what the hell difference does it make? They're still dead!"

He answered, "It doesn't make any difference to me, but I guess it does to Dad, because that's what he wants you to do. Now, you do what you want to, but if you're smart, you'll stomp those worms."

I must have been the most gullible child in the world, because I threw the stick down and raised my foot to kill the first worm. Picking up my foot was easy, but lowering it on a fat, juicy worm, was not. When my toes almost touched the worm, my foot would automatically draw back. I finally shut my eyes and put my foot down hard. I spent the next five minutes cleaning that gooey mess off my foot, in the dirt. Killing the second worm was a little easier, but it was a really bad morning of stomping and cleaning; stomping and cleaning.

We finally went to the house for lunch. When I saw Dad, I proudly began telling him how many worms I had stomped that morning.

He said, "I don't know what you're talking about, Dan."

I asked, "Well, didn't you leave word with Rex for me to stomp those worms in the cotton?"

"No," he replied.

"Well, Rex said you did!"

"Why, I didn't do any such of a thing. I didn't tell him to have you kill them with a stick, your foot, or anything else."

When we were alone, I promised my brother that he would die a slow, painful death in the very near future, but I never got around to keeping my vow.

Chapter 3

Tenny Shoes

This story is about "tenny shoes." I learned later in life there was a game called tennis. I'm sure those shoes were named after the game, but I called them tenny shoes.

As a five year old, I had little need for shoes of any kind during warm weather. After going barefoot all summer, my feet were so tough that I could run across rocks and sparks would fly.

Fall came, and a chill was in the air. My older brothers had tenny shoes to wear to school. They were the old time, cheap, high topped ones: the kind that kids started wearing again a few years ago because they thought they were cool. They made your feet hot, sweaty and smelly. The main reason I wanted some was so my feet would stink as bad as my brothers'.

I begged, pleaded and cried for some, so finally the folks scraped up enough money to buy a pair for me. I was so proud of them! I raced around, showing my brothers Rex and J.C. how fast I could run in my new shoes.

Rex, the brother who delighted in getting me into trouble, said, "My Goodness alive, as fast as you can run, there's no need for you to ever get another whipping. You can outrun Mama as easy as pie. If I were you, the next time she started to whip me, I'd just take off running." It sounded like a good idea to me.

My mother was the sweetest lady in the world, but it seemed to me that she divided her time equally between washing clothes on a rub board, ironing with an old sad iron (which she set on top of the stove to heat), cooking on a wood stove and whipping me. She didn't whip me very hard, but I learned when I was very young, that the louder I yelled, the shorter the duration of the whipping. Consequently, I developed pretty good lungs, screaming my head off when she whipped me. I could have put a howler monkey to shame!

One morning, soon after I got my tenny shoes, Mama was outdoors, washing clothes in a tub. I was racing around, showing off my speed, and accidentally kicked a little dirt into the wash tub. Mama took exception to that. She grabbed a little stick and started after me, so I just threw my head back and ran off that hill like a bullet, bouncing from rock to rock. I looked back, and she had not chased me very far.

She hollered and told me, "You're making a bad mistake! You'd better come on back and take your medicine."

That didn't make any sense, whatsoever to me, so I just kept hauling ass. I ran about a half-a-mile down to the creek and messed around for what seemed like many hours. Hunger pangs began to cause me to forget the problems at home, and surely Mama would not remember what had happened so long ago. I began to feel confident that I could ease back to the house, keep an eye on Mama, just in case she hadn't forgotten it, and everything would be all right. I did just that, watching Mama out of the corner of my eye; and she seemed not to notice that her long lost child had returned. I relaxed a little bit; but all of a sudden, I realized that Mama had two things in her hands. One was a big leather belt, and the other was my left arm.

She said, "O.K. young man, this one is for kicking dirt into the wash tub."

She did blister my behind! Howling didn't do much good, that day. She gave me a dandy. She finished that whipping and said, "Now, this one is for running away from me." She literally beat the tar out of me that time!

I never thought about running from her again. If Mama were alive today, she would be over 100 years old; but if for any reason, she started after me with a stick—"Do you think I'd run? Hell, no, I learned my lesson!"

Chapter 4

Cash for Crawfish

A long time ago, there was a deep hole of water in Spring Creek north of Camp Springs, Texas, called the baptizin' hole. It was fed by springs, and the water was cool and clear; but things have changed. Nearly seventy years have passed, and time and erosion have taken their toll. The springs have dried up and the water hole is full of silt.

I recall when the baptizin' hole served several purposes. First, it was the baptistery for the Camp Springs Baptist Church. When the church received new members, they waited for a warm Sunday afternoon and baptized them by immersing them in the creek. That was an important social event for me. My folks belonged to the Methodist Church, where "coming to Jesus" preceded baptism by sprinkling; so I was always at the creek to see how long the Baptist preacher held them under the water.

The second function, as far as I was concerned, was far more important than baptism. It was the swimming hole for the boys in the community. When someone was to be baptized, the preacher sent some of the men ahead to chase the naked boys out of the creek. The congregation then followed. That is where I learned to swim. It wasn't too difficult to learn after my brother tossed me in the creek and said, "Swim or drown!"

The third, and most important purpose, for me; it was my private place to catch crawfish. That was one of the most fun things I did when I was about five years old.

The days I went for crawfish, my mother fixed a lunch for me to take to the creek. It was a mile from home, so I usually made a day of it. Mama would get out the sow belly and cut off a small strip of the rind, which I tied to a piece of twine. That was my fishing bait and tackle. Then I loaded my stuff, including a bucket for the crawfish, in my red wagon; whistled for my dog Popeye, and together, we hit the road. Those were wonderful days, spent alone, with nobody hassling me. When I got to the baptizin' hole, I'd lower the bacon rind into the water around the rocks, and the crawfish would catch the bait in their pinchers. If I pulled it up slowly and carefully, they continued to hang on. I lifted them out on the bank, caught them and put them into the bucket. I spent many an hour there, pulling crawfish out of the water.

Once in a great while, I could talk my mother into frying some of the crawfish tails for me. She didn't do it many times because she hated to peel and cook those things about as bad as she hated to cook a rabbit. I thought they were delicious. They were a tasty change from the pork and beef to which we were accustomed at every meal. I didn't know anyone else who ate crawfish back in those days; and certainly, I had no idea that they would become a delicacy in later years. If Mama refused to cook them, I kept them in a tank and played with them until they died.

One day I was sitting on the bank, fishing for crawfish, when a strange man came walking down the trail. He told me that he lived in Snyder, which was about fifteen miles away. He said he was going fishing the next week and asked if I would sell the bucket of crawfish I had caught. He wanted them for bait. I didn't like his idea very well; I was not sure I wanted him to use them for bait. We kept dickering over a price, until he finally offered me a quarter for all the crawfish I had in the bucket. I had caught a big black one that I was really proud of, and I refused to include it in the twenty-five cent deal. The man kept pressuring me to sell it and finally offered a nickel for the big one. I took it! I had thirty cents! I had never had that much money before. I thought that man was the richest, craziest person I had ever seen.

I went by the local store, bought some candy, and went home jingling money in my pocket. I'm sure it must have crossed Mama's mind that I might have burglarized a couple of businesses in order to get that much money. When I told her what had happened, she agreed that the man was goofy and had probably escaped from an asylum.

I sat on that same rock by the creek for many, many hours afterward, occasionally glancing up the trail, hoping the crawfish buyer just might come back with some more "cash money." I never saw him again, but I had pulled off my first big financial deal!

Chapter 5

Cross-Dressing

December 12, 1931 was probably not a special day for very many folks, but it was for me. It was my birthday. Mama had cooked a red devil's food cake with white icing and put five candles on it. That made it special. We never received gifts on birthdays; mostly, I guess because there was very little money for Christmas, much less birthdays. However, we always had cake. The birthday present from each of my brothers and my sister was several hard smacks on the seat of my pants; one for each year of my age.

A couple of weeks later, Christmas morning came; and I could hardly believe it, but Santa Claus had brought me a fifty shot Daisy air rifle. It was a dandy! It was not one of those little plinkers that would shoot about thirty feet. It was a hard shooting gun, and I quickly became a crack shot with it. We had feed for the livestock around the place, so there were always birds to be shot; and a sparrow that sat still for two minutes was at risk. There's no telling how many birds I killed with that gun. We also had a lot of cottontail rabbits in the catclaw bushes on the hill behind our house. I learned that if I were as quiet as an Indian, I was able to sneak up close to the rabbits and dispatch them with a couple of well placed shots. I thinned out the rabbits on that rocky hill. Sometimes, I carried a young one to the house for Mama to cook. A lot of people ate rabbits during those hard times, but our family didn't. I believe my mother thought it was degrading to eat them so I was not able to convince her to cook one very often.

I had earned the reputation, among our relatives, of being pretty handy with my gun; so I shouldn't have been too surprised when my Aunt Lilly, Uncle Will Talley, and their sixteen-year-old daughter Grace, came to our house to offer me a job. They had a beautiful garden, lots of flowers and fruit trees. They had a lot of fruit that year; but as it started to ripen, the birds moved in and were eating it up.

The Talleys were some of my favorite relatives, and I was always eager to go to their house and this time they asked me to go home with them for two or three days and kill birds. I probably would have done it for fun; but they said they would pay me a penny for each bird I killed, so I jumped at the chance. I loaded up with ammunition (two tubes of bee-bees) at the local store. When we arrived at their place, I loaded up my gun, went to the orchard, shot twenty birds in less than an hour, threw my gun over my shoulder and went to the house.

Aunt Lilly and Uncle Will met me at the door and asked, "Dan, why aren't you shooting birds?"

I replied, "I'm tired; and it's hot out there. Besides, I killed twenty. Do you want to see 'em?"

They were a bit upset, explaining, "We made a deal with you to kill the birds that are ruining our fruit. Will you please go shoot some more birds? You know, you can make more money."

"Nope," I said, "I'm gonna' rest a while, and twenty cents is all the money I need."

Finally, they prevailed on me to go back to work. I killed a lot of birds in a couple of days and got them thinned out enough to save the fruit. The Talleys were happy; and so was I, since I had made some good money.

I was the youngest child among our friends and relatives; so I was "picked" at and sometimes tormented from the time I was a year old until I was nearly grown.

The last night I spent with Aunt Lilly and Uncle Will during the bird exterminating campaign, I fell asleep on the couch in the living room. When I awoke the next morning, I discovered that they had undressed me and put me to bed wearing one of Grace's nightgowns. I threw the damnedest fit that anyone in that family had ever witnessed. I screamed and used words they had not heard many times. I kicked things and totally disrupted their tranquil household. They thought it was awfully funny, but they never even thought about putting another nightgown on me!

Chapter 6

Kissing Lil' Stanford

I was born fifteen miles east of Snyder, Texas, in the thriving metropolis of Camp Springs. It boasted of two grocery stores, one of which had the Post Office in it, a gas station, a blacksmith shop and a cotton gin. Camp Springs also had a small two-teacher school house where they taught children through the sixth grade. I started to school there in 1932 at the age of five.

My sister and two brothers were in high school, so they rode a rickety old school bus to school at Hobbs, Texas, which was six miles east of where we lived. As a five-year-old, first grader, I had to walk a mile west, alone, to school at Camp Springs. It was an awfully long, lonesome walk for me. I felt I was the most mistreated child in the world.

The first grade was dismissed early each day, but we were required to stay on the school grounds until all classes were dismissed. About a half dozen children were in my class, and I remember one little boy named Stanford Thomas. He was what I'd call a "hitter." He was just a pain in my ass. He didn't hurt me when he hit me, because he hit like a girl; so I thought he was kind of sissy. He was always tappin' around on me; and after a few days, I decided it was time to stop that.

We were playing outside one afternoon, and he hit me; so I just reached down about my knee, came up with a "round-house-right" and smacked him in the left eye as hard as I could. I have never heard a kid scream as loud in my life. He could have been heard three miles down the road, screaming, "Oh, my eyeball's busted!" All that screaming scared hell out of me and I wondered if I had hit him too hard. Our teacher, Mrs. Cook, came out of the school house door like the tail of her dress was on fire. She was in an awful rush to see if little Stanford's eyeball was actually busted. He was still screaming his head off; but after she had determined that it was not life threatening, she grabbed me by the arm and took us both inside the school and kept us until school turned out. After all the other children were gone, she got out a scary looking old strap that looked like the tug off a set of harness. That big strap looked awfully menacing to me, as a child. She waved it around quite a bit and talked about little boys who fought, looking at me most of the time, because little Stanford hadn't done much fighting.

I was scared to death, but I happened to look out the window and saw my folks riding by in a wagon pulled by a team of mules. We didn't have a car at the time. That was during the depression, and our old car had "froze and busted," so we hadn't had one for several years. I thought, "Oh man, I've missed my ride home." I knew my folks would notice that school was out and think I had gone home. I have an idea that Mrs. Cook saw them passing, too, because suddenly, she said, "Dan, if you'll kiss Stanford, I'll excuse you."

Well, man, I grabbed little Stanford and gave him a big smack on the cheek and hit that door in a dead run. By the way, I caught the wagon. The folks wanted to know where the rest of the kids were, and I said, "Well, they got out a little early."

When we lined up on the benches around the supper table at night, that's when all the crap came out. If anybody had anything to share or something on his mind, that was when he brought it up.

A few nights after the kissing incident, during supper, they started grilling me.

Someone asked, "How's school, Dan?"

I answered, "Fine!"

"Do you like Johnny?"

"Oh, he's my best friend."

"How about Jimmy?"

"Well, he's all right."

After a little more conversation, the question I had been dreading came out!

"How about Stanford Thomas? Do you like him?"

"I like him fine."

"You don't ever have any trouble with him?"

"No, I don't ever have any trouble with anybody."

"You never did hit lil' Stanford in the eye?"

"No."

"You never did kiss lil' Stanford?"

"Of course not. Boys don't kiss boys."

"You're sure you never kissed him?"

"I'm positive."

They continued this third degree, doing everything but putting thumb screws on me. I certainly hadn't told anyone. I doubt that lil' Stanford did, so I imagine Mrs. Cook decided that it was too good to keep and shared that tidbit with some of my folks.

I didn't admit that I had kissed that kid until I was twenty-one years old. That incident didn't change my life; but I can't speak for Stanford, because I lost track of him. I just hope it didn't have an adverse effect on his personality. A modern psychiatrist would probably have a field day with this.

CHAPTER 7

The Pitching Jackass

My mother told me that when I was just a baby, my two brothers (J.C. and Rex) traded for an old jackass that was a pitching son of a bitch. He bucked them off regularly, and eventually pretty well got his bluff in on them. He would buck anywhere, but there was one particular place where he rounded the corner of the corral, that he always unloaded his pack. When this happened, Dad would laugh and say, "Get up and get back on him. I wouldn't let a little old mule get his bluff in on me!" My mother got awfully tired of hearing him say that, and so did the boys. The mule had thrown them so many times they were getting kind of scared of him.

One day J.C. rode the donkey up to the field where Dad was harrowing some new ground. Dad had gathered up a bunch of mesquite stumps and piled them at the end of the rows, with the idea of carrying them to the house to burn for fuel in the cook stove. It was quitting time, and Dad had been walking behind the harrow for fourteen hours; so it was not too hard for J.C. to talk him into riding the donkey back to the house and letting him drive Dad's team of mules.

Dad got on the donkey, and J.C. handed him the armload of stumps. When they got to the house, Dad had forgotten about the place where the jackass always started pitching. Sure enough, just as the old donkey turned the corner of the corral, he cut loose to bucking. Dad said later that the first jump loosened him up, and the second one threw him and the stumps ten feet into the air. He landed on his back, on top of one of the mesquite stumps. He thought he was badly injured; maybe a kidney was knocked loose.

My mother was standing on the porch watching what was taking place. As I said before, she was tired of Dad telling the boys to "get up and get back on the donkey." She yelled, "Get up and get back on him, I wouldn't let a little old mule bluff me!"

She said later that if she had known Dad was lying dead in the yard, she would have said the same thing.

There was a happier ending to that part of the story. They took Dad to town to see a doctor, thinking he was seriously injured; but by the time the old Model-T Ford had shook him around for fifteen miles over a rough dirt road, he decided he was OK.

J.C. and Rex sold the old jackass to a guy from Fluvanna, Texas, who showed up to get him one morning with a saddle and wearing a ten gallon hat, boots and spurs. That kind of garb for riding a jackass was unheard of. The customary way to ride one was to ride bareback, and sit back toward the donkey's rear end.

The boys watched the "cowboy" saddle the old mule, and were quite amused at the way he was rigged up. He looked like Tom Mix, riding a donkey. They gleefully watched the old donkey bust his ass a couple of times before he got away from the house.

Later in the day, some of our folks saw the donkey tied to a post across the road from the local store, which was a mile and a half from where we lived. Their curiosity got the best of them; so they asked the folks at the store about the jackass rider. He had borrowed their telephone and called a friend to bring a trailer to haul the old donkey to Fluvanna, which was about twenty-five miles away. They heard him say, "That damned jackass has bucked me off thirteen times in a mile and a half!"

J.C. and Rex took an awful lot of comfort in the fact that they were not the only ones the old donkey had bucked off so many times.

Chapter 8

The Purple Pencil

In the fall of 1934, before my eighth birthday, I was invited to go on a long, exciting trip. I remember it almost as clearly as if it were yesterday. It was a very important event in my life.

My sister, Bargy, was teaching school in the very remote community, County Line, a two teacher school, located in the northwest corner of Fisher County, Texas. I went to school at Hobbs, Texas, about ten miles south of County Line.

Bargy had invited me to come and spend a weekend with her. The night before I was to leave, Mama cornered me and forced me to take a bath in the galvanized tin, No. 3 wash tub. She checked my neck and ears to be sure I had washed them. Later, we packed a small sack with clean clothes.

When I got on my school bus the next morning, I was shining like new money. After school, I was to catch the school bus that went north toward County Line.

Physically, I was in school that day, but my mind kept wandering. Would I be able to find the right bus? Would I know for sure where to get off? Would I be able to find Bargy's house before dark? If I didn't, would the coyotes and mountain lions get me? I had been to Bargy's house once, but it seemed so far away. We didn't travel very far from home in those days. We had no car for a long time because the motor in our Model T Ford had frozen and busted the block. Dad did not have the money to fix it, so we traveled by horseback, wagon, or on foot.

The bell finally rang, signaling that school was out. I found the right bus, got on and headed for County Line. Outwardly, I was calm, but inside I was plenty nervous! The same things I had worried about all day kept returning to my mind.

I rode the bus to the end of the line, got off and started hoofing it. I hitched a ride for a couple of miles, and then started burning shoe leather again. As I walked, I thought about how wonderful my sister was and how good she had been to me.

Bargy graduated from Hobbs High School in 1932 with a burning desire to further her education. Her dream was to go to McMurry College in Abilene, Texas and become a school teacher. My folks had told her they could not afford to send her to college. However, the day before the fall semester started, my dad came to the house and said, "Margie (that was her real name), do you really want to go to college?

She answered, "Oh My Goodness, yes!"

Dad said, "There's a cow trader out here who has offered me $12.50 for a good fat cow, and that will pay the tuition; so if you're sure you want to go, I'm gonna' sell that cow."

She started to school at McMurry the next day! At that time, anyone could get a teaching certificate (for smaller schools) after two years of college. She completed the two years and applied for a job at County Line, knowing she would receive her certificate and become eighteen years of age just in time to teach when school started in October. The school board hired her but then decided to start school a month early, in September. Bargy met with them, confessed that she would not receive her teaching certificate until October, but would work without pay until then. They agreed. Her salary was $60.00 a month. Some schools did not have the money to meet the payroll, so they issued script to the teachers. It was sort of an IOU, and most of the time it could be sold at a discount; but I believe Bargy got her check most of the time.

At the time of my visit, she had been paid and had a little cash. Money was a scarce commodity around our house at that time. The country was trying to recover from the Great Depression, and we were in a very serious two-year drouth. My mother was not well, so there were plenty of reasons why we were barely "getting by."

Bargy boarded with the Poteet family; and just before sundown, I was relieved to see their house at a distance. As I neared, I could see Bargy waiting on the porch for me! I'm sure my shoulders straightened and my step became lighter. It had been a long day. I was proud of myself and so glad to see my sister!

Dan and his sister Bargy, during a visit with her in 1934.

That night Bargy told me that we were going to Rotan the next day, with the Poteets, so I was up at daylight, getting dressed for the trip. It was the most wonderful day I had ever had. Bargy bought big hamburgers and Coca Colas for our lunch; and lots of ice cream and candy. It was the first time I had ever had all I could eat of those things. What a day!! But, the most exciting gift was yet to come. She bought an Eversharp mechanical pencil for me! I had never seen one before. It had a purple, hexagon shaped barrel, and I have never owned anything I was as proud of. Needless to say, I did lots of writing that night and the next day.

Monday morning, at daylight, I retraced my steps toward Hobbs with the purple pencil in my pocket. I could hardly wait to get to school. I showed that pencil to everyone. There was not another one like it, but I scratched my initials in the paint anyway, and I was the envy of every kid in school.

A few days passed, and my pencil disappeared. It had cost twenty-five cents; I knew I couldn't get another one, and I was just sick. Shortly after the pencil disappeared, a boy in my class came to school with a beautiful purple pencil exactly like mine—same color, same everything. The only difference was that his pencil had a shiny place on the barrel where my initials had been, and his name was scratched in a different place. I threw a wall-eyed fit! The teacher, Miss Bennet, heard the ruckus, and I explained that this was my lost pencil and I intended to get it back.

The kid was yelling, "No, my dad bought this pencil for me, and he will tell you he did."

Miss Bennet knew it was mine and said, "Since your father is the school janitor and here in the building, we'll just ask him."

She thought the boy would back down and that would solve the problem. However, that is not what happened.

The father came in and said, "I bought that pencil for him; it's his, and I want him to have it."

Everyone in the room knew he was lying, but the only thing the teacher could do was to give the pencil to the other boy. I didn't feel that was all I could do. I waited until recess, got him behind the outhouse, whipped his ass, took the pencil away from him, put it in my pocket, and went back to class. That settled the pencil issue. It was never mentioned again.

I've wondered many times what happened to a boy whose father would lie for him in front of a bunch of third grade kids.

Chapter 9

Pee and Poetry

It was a hot day in the rural community of Lloyd Mountain, located fifteen miles Northeast of Snyder, Texas, in late July of 1937. The highest temperature ever recorded in the State of Texas had occurred at Seymour the year before. The mercury had hit one hundred twenty degrees, and as a hot, tired ten-year-old, I was sure it would set a new record that day. Not a leaf had moved that morning in the mesquite brush where I rode horseback, looking for wormy cattle. This was long before the Screw Worm Eradication Program, and the slightest scratch on an animal could result in a case of screw worms. This caused severe weight loss, and occasional death of young animals. Livestock had to be checked at least twice a week.

I had come to the house to eat and change horses. Rex, my nineteen-year-old brother, was there to refuel the John Deere tractor. He would be plowing more weeds out of the cotton that afternoon. Dad had been plowing feed with a team of mules; so he was as tired, hungry and thirsty as the rest of us when we met in Mama's kitchen to eat.

My mother had cooked a good lunch, as usual, and announced that we were having iced tea with "dinner" (as we called it). On Saturday, Dad had gone to town and returned with a fifty-pound block of ice. We had carefully wrapped it in an old quilt and a tarpaulin, since we had no ice box. We had made ice cream on Sunday and enjoyed tea with every meal, so I assumed that the rest of the ice had melted; but Mama had found enough ice in the old quilt for tea for dinner that day. What a wonderful surprise!

After dinner my Dad got his old, straight backed, cowhide

bottomed chair and turned it upside down on the living room floor so that he could lean back on it for a nap. Mama did not allow anyone to lie on the beds until we cleaned up at night.

Dad had just dozed off when my sister, Marguerite Hargrove, whom we called Bargy, drove up. She had come to tell us she had been hired as one of the two teachers at the Lloyd Mountain school, starting in September.

The country was just beginning to recover from the Great Depression. Cash was scarce; and better paying jobs, such as teaching, were hard to come by. Bargy was ecstatic, and so was the rest of the family. I was less enthusiastic than the rest because this meant that she would be my teacher for nine, long months. She had married by this time, but the family decided that she would stay with us during the week, and return home to her husband on weekends. Since the small, red brick school building was located on the corner of our place, this meant we would even walk to school together.

Mama, Dad and Bargy were my three favorite people in the world. My sister claimed to have carried me, as a child, on her hip until my feet dragged the ground, so I guess our close feelings were mutual. However, what I did not need was a twenty-four-hour-a-day teacher! She was a strict disciplinarian, and as the saying goes,

Red brick schoolhouse where Bargy taught Dan.

"didn't put up with any crap!" Having been reared with three brothers, she was as tough as a pig's nose. My Dad, knowing that one of my great pleasures in life was increasing the excitement level of my teachers, explained to me that I would toe the line at school. He felt sure that Bargy could handle any situation that might arise; but, if not, he would skin me alive when I got home. Dad always meant business.

The school building was used for all the social, religious and educational activities in the community. The local Church of Christ held services there every Sunday. Almost everyone in the community belonged to this church (except my family). We were Methodist; and when we first moved into the community, we attended church services at the school for three or four Sundays. This didn't work out too well, so my parents quit going. I continued to go to church most Sundays, not because of a strong religious conviction, but because there were usually two or three good fist fights either before, during or after the services. During school one got in trouble for fighting, but on Sunday everything was fair; and I enjoyed going down and scrapping with the kids.

The summer days flew by; fall came and school started. It soon became a series of confrontations between Bargy and me. We tried to keep them minor, because I didn't want Dad to get involved, and neither did my sister.

The school year wore on, and one dull afternoon, during English class, I was sitting, daydreaming about whipping up on a whole tribe of Indians, when suddenly, something was said that attracted my attention. I thought, "What in the world did Bargy say?" Then it dawned on me that she was assigning the next day's lesson. Each student was supposed to write eight lines of poetry. I thought, "What in the world has possessed her? She must have lost her mind!" I was a cowboy. Nowadays it's popular for cowboys to write poetry, and many of them do; but back then, cowboys didn't read poetry, much less write it. I didn't even go to see Roy Rogers or Gene Autry at the picture show, because they played the guitar; and once in a while, one of them even acted like he wanted to kiss the girl. So I certainly didn't believe in reading or writing poetry. That was sissy stuff!

The next day she called on each one to read their poem, and everyone did. When my turn came, she said, "Let's hear yours, Dan."

I said, "I don't have one."

She said, "You'll have one when you leave here!"

I thought, "Well, sister, you'd better be prepared for a long, long wait."

We sat there and sat there after school; and after a couple or three hours at least, the sun began to set over Lloyd Mountain, west of the school. I began to get a little nervous. I knew my dad was going to be looking down the road to see where in the world I was; because the cows weren't gathered up to be milked, and the horses and hogs weren't fed. I knew someone was going to be in a helluva lot of trouble, and I was certain who that "someone" was. I'm sure that Bargy realized the same thing, so I don't know who made the first suggestion for a subject for a poem; but I'll bet it was my sister. I jumped on it pretty quickly, and together we wrote a poem. It was not a good poem but I'd give anything in this world if we had saved it for posterity. At least it was a poem, and I stood up in school the next day and read it. I was never so embarrassed in my life.

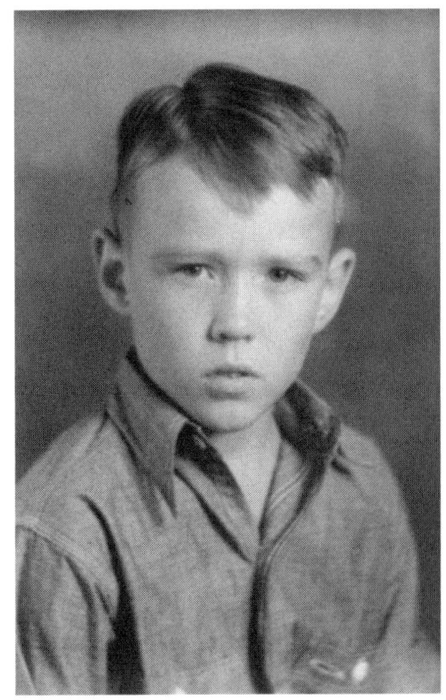

Dan contemplating revenge against sister/teacher Bargy for poetry assignment and other burdens.

That was the worst school year I had ever been through and I spent a fair amount of time figuring how I could repay her for all the indignities I had suffered.

Fall turned into winter; and as the days grew colder, a wonderful plan of repayment was forming in my mind!

The school building was heated by a large, oil-burning stove. Attached to the back was a small tank for water to humidify the air. Each morning, Bargy and I went to school early to start the fire; and by the time all the kids got there, that old stove was hotter than a blazing stump.

I had found a way to slip into the school building at night. I did this on a number of occasions, poured the water out of the tank on the old stove and PEED in it.

There is no way to describe the terrible odor in the room when that stove got hot. Opening doors and windows helped some, but not much. "Furious" is too mild a term to describe my sister's reaction. She threatened whoever was responsible with the most terrible means of slow death that she could think of.

I was most pleased with my creative prank; but this was becoming dangerous. I knew if I was ever suspected, I would never see my eleventh birthday. However, it was so much fun that I just had to do it one more time. This time I gave it a double shot. They had to dismiss school!

I had seen my sister mad many, many times; but this time she literally went crazy. She asked God for a name. Thank goodness He didn't provide it.

Even after this eventful year with Bargy as my teacher, she was still the dearest person in the world to me.

Fifty years later, we were reminiscing; and she got mad again when the subject of dismissing school came up. She said, "I know who did it. It was that Tom Frank Forrest, and it's a good thing for him that I couldn't prove it."

I said, "No, Bargy, you're wrong."

She said, "How do you know?"

I said, "Because I can scratch the rear of the guy who did it."

No cursing, no screaming, no hair pulling, she just said, "Oh"!

It was never mentioned again.

PART II

Ranching and Farming Near Colorado City, Texas

Chapter 10

A Smiling Horse

When I was ten years old, my Dad traded for a big paint, thoroughbred type horse that was a pretty fair cow pony. We immediately dubbed him "Old Paint." Dad didn't buy many good saddle horses; he preferred to buy a cheaper one and have me make a better one out of him. I believe he thought this was good for both me and the horse, since it kept me busy and increased the value of the horse.

I was riding the paint one day and needed to cross the fence into another pasture. The nearest gate was a long way off; so, although I knew better, I decided to take a short cut. I kicked the staples out of a couple of fence posts, which allowed me to push the barbed wires down with my foot to about knee high. I started to lead the horse over the fence; but when he got his front feet across, he bumped me, which caused my foot to slip off the wires. When the tightly stretched wires hit him, the frightened horse ran backward, dragging his foot across the barbed wire and almost severing a fore foot. It took a long time to lead him back home on the bad foot. All the way home I was thinking that Dad would probably beat me to death; but when I told him, he didn't say a word. He just looked sick and went to the barn to doctor the horse.

Months passed before Old Paint was able to be ridden again. The first time I saddled him up and got on, I had quite a surprise. He rared up on his hind legs. This was a little scary for me because it was possible that he might fall backward and land on top of me. Dad was watching, and I'm sure that it scared him more than it did me; so he went to the tractor shed, got a pick handle, and sawed it off, shortening it up a bit. He drilled a hole in it and put a leather string through it for my wrist so that I could have both hands free when necessary.

Dad never saw the movie "The Horse Whisperer," so he didn't know about whispering in a horse's ear, nor did he realize the need for staring down a horse. He was from the old school of horse training; a man of action, tough, and his voice was loud and clear when he said, "Dan, I want you to take this club, get back on that horse and when he starts to rare up, you stand up in the stirrups and hit that old bastard right between the ears. If you knock him down two or three times, I think you can stop him from getting a bad habit; but if you kill him it's O.K."

I climbed on and did exactly as Dad said. I nudged Old Paint with a spur; but this time when his front feet left the ground, I was ready. I stood up in the stirrups and laid that pick handle squarely between his ears with everything I had. Kersplat! His knees sagged a little, but he didn't go down. This continued five or six times; and each time the horse rared up, I stroked his head with the club. I was

Dan got this Pottsingerton saddle, made in Amarillo, in the 1940s. After spending "half his life" in this saddle, he has put it "out to pasture" in his home.

never able to knock him completely down; I was just too light in the seat of the pants. Finally, Dad told me to get off, and he pulled the saddle off Old Paint. He said, "Don't ever get on this horse again and don't let anybody else ride him; he'll hurt somebody. We'll make a work horse out of him."

We kept him for several years; and many times, when my folks were gone and I wanted a little excitement, I'd get the pick handle and saddle up the old paint horse. I guess I mostly rode him because I wasn't supposed to. I never broke him from his dangerous habit; but as I got older and stronger and could massage his head with a little more gusto, he and I had an understanding. He would rare up a few times when we left the barn, and then we would go to work.

The last time I rode Old Paint, a friend and I were looking for some cows along a creek when "Lo and Behold," we spotted an armadillo. We quickly tied our horses and took after that armadillo in earnest. We had quite a time of it; but, amazingly, we caught him. What a prize! I had never seen more than a couple of them before and certainly had not been able to capture one. We quickly abandoned the idea of checking cattle and started home with our new-found friend. I was holding him by the tail, at arms length, when all of a sudden Old Paint "broke in two." About the second jump he made, I was literally catapulted from the saddle. I went so high that I was sure I could see everything within a two mile radius; and somewhere in mid-air, the armadillo and I passed each other. When I hit the ground, the lights went out for me; but a bit later, when I began to get some air back into my lungs; I realized what had happened. As I carried the armadillo, my arm had become tired, and I had gradually lowered him until he got his long claws into the horse's flank. That's when Old Paint came unfrazzled! I was rubbing a big knot on my head when I heard my friend say, "I caught your horse."

I asked, "Where's the armadillo?"

"He's gone!" he replied.

I opened my eyes, and there stood Old Paint. He cut his eyes toward me and tried to look serious, but I know I saw him smile!

Chapter 11

Rodeo Parade

When I was about 13 years old, a neighbor kid and I decided we would ride in the rodeo parade at Colorado City, Texas. This was pretty big doings for a couple of towheaded kids.

On the morning of the parade, we saddled up and headed for town, about six miles away. We were really excited because neither of us had ever done anything like that before. We got to Colorado City about lunch time, found a place where we could tie our horses, and headed for Hardegree's Hamburger Joint. We ate a ten-cent hamburger and drank a nickel Coca-Cola. What a meal! Then, we got back on our horses and started looking around town. There was plenty to see, but a lot more for the horses to look at. Mind you, they were country horses, with plenty of things to "booger" them in this busy town. Cars were honking, people yelling, and kids running everywhere. My horse didn't like what was going on around him, but my friend's horse was really getting jumpy. I realized that my friend was scared of his old pony; because, he talked me into trading horses with him before the parade started. I don't guess I had enough sense to be afraid of his horse.

What an exciting time! Things went well enough during the parade, even though fire trucks were blowing their sirens, bands were playing, and every car, pickup, and truck in the parade was honking its horn. It was an experience for both of us boys that we would not soon forget. We were real cowboys and were really "rared back" in the saddle as we rode along with a hundred other cowboys.

When the parade was over, everyone was trying to leave town at the same time; and during the melee, my friend and I became

Dan's "working" boots, complete with Crockett antique spurs.

separated. I was easing around downtown, looking for my partner. I was on the right side of the street, riding between the rear end of the parked cars and the traffic, in sort of close quarters. A lot of gravel was on the pavement, and my friend's horse, that I was still riding, was getting plenty spooky.

All of a sudden, a boy with a bicycle, pushed it out from between two parked cars and shoved it right under the nose of my excited horse. The bicycle had streamers hanging all over it, and the wheels were completely encircled with crepe paper. It was a wild looking "set of wheels." Being a country horse and never having been to town before, he sure as hell had never seen anything like that. His eyeballs nearly jumped out of their sockets! I never saw a horse come unfrazzled much quicker than he did. He just threw a walleyed fit. He tried to run backward and sideways, at the same time, to get away from the bicycle; but his feet flew out from under him.

I had no time to get off of him, so together we rolled around in the gravel for quite a while. He skinned me up from head to toe—

there was hardly a spot on me that was not peeled. I really would have liked to have thrashed the daylights out of the boy with the bicycle, but I had about all I could handle with the horse and the traffic.

I finally found my friend, got on my own horse, and we headed for home. What a day it had been for two kids. I looked like a wild cat had had a hold of me, but it was worth it. We felt as big as any two full grown cowboys. I never had a desire, however, to ride in another parade.

Chapter 12

Shooting Star

When I was fourteen years old, I had a dandy, chestnut sorrel, Spanish type pony. He had a white spot on his forehead, so naturally, I called him Star. He was an exceptionally good cow horse, but hell to pen. I never knew whether it was because he hated to be ridden or because he enjoyed the game of "pen the pony." Most horses could be tolled into the pen with feed, but not the Star horse. I'll bet I chased him several hundred miles on foot, which may be the reason I have such a bad disposition today.

Once my mother and dad went to town early one morning, and Dad told me to check some cattle while they were gone. Old Star was in the trap behind the barn when I went out to drive him into the pen. He led me right down to the gate, then threw up his tail and hauled ass for the backside of the trap. I followed him and drove him back again. The same thing happened. That happened over and over and over for at least three hours. I got to the point where I was just running and cussing and crying.

I went to the house and got an old Long Tom single-barreled shotgun that belonged to my dad, loaded it up and went back to the trap.

I said, "Star, you son of a bitch, I'm gonna' give you one more chance."

I drove him back to the corral gate again; and as I approached it to drive him through, the same thing happened as before. He threw his tail up one more time and headed for the backside of the trap. I raised the gun to my shoulder, took careful aim at his rear end and pulled the trigger, but because of my anger and the tears in my eyes,

I was not able to judge the distance very well.

I never moved out of my tracks after I shot him; but old Star looked like 'Whirlaway' as he picked up speed, running around the trap, and I could tell he was headed for the gate. However, when he got about three fourths of the way around, he began to slow down. As he got closer to the gate, he moved slower and slower. His legs were stiffening up and he was beginning to limp badly. By the time he got into the corral, he could barely walk. I knew by then that I had made a terrible mistake. I was a little bit sick at my stomach, so I just went to the house and sat down, hoping it would be a long time before Dad got home.

I was still sitting there when Mom and Dad came in. Dad asked, "How do the cattle look in the west pasture?"

I muttered, "I don't know."

He asked, "Why don't you know?"

I replied, "Old Star is lame, so I couldn't check on them."

Dad headed for the barn to look at the horse. I was sort of lingering behind him when he asked, "What seems to be his problem?"

I could hardly get the words out of my mouth, but I said, "I shot him."

Godamighty! Dad jumped four feet in the air and yelled, "You what?"

I told him again, and I thought he was going to faint. We looked at the horse and everywhere a shot had hit him there was a little blood oozing out.

That was the maddest I had ever seen Dad, but he was a hell of a lot madder when I told him, "Star is my horse and I'll shoot him if I want to." That statement was an awfully bad mistake.

A couple of weeks later, Star and I were both OK and he was a lot easier to pen. In later years when he got a little hard to drive into the corral, I grabbed up a stick, threw it to my shoulder like a gun, and old Star started looking for a gate.

Chapter 13

A Spanking

When I started my senior year in high school at Colorado City, Texas, one of the subjects I had signed up for was Spanish 2. I had taken Spanish 1 the year before and liked it for two reasons. I enjoyed the subject and my friend Pete and I were Miss Mable Smith's pets. She had taught Spanish there forever, but shortly after my senior year started, she left.

The school hired a young lady by the name of Donaldson. She was barely out of college, probably not over 19 or 20 years old, and didn't weigh a hundred pounds soaking wet. She was a nice young lady, but I suppose I resented her because I had been Miss Smith's pet, and that was not the case with Miss Donaldson. She treated me just as she treated everyone else in the class. I stayed in her class for a short time, then dropped Spanish 2. I'm quite sure that she resented the fact that I had dropped the class and possibly realized the reason, so we were not the best of friends for a while. After a time, however, I really liked her, and I think the feeling was mutual.

She took her lunch break during the period before noon, then came back and watched over the study hall during the noon hour. She drove an old, gray, 1936 Plymouth coupe; and one morning before school, I rigged one of those old smoking, whistling, popping bombs on her car. Somehow, the word got out; so when she started to leave for her lunch break, it so happened that every kid in school was up sharpening a pencil or had some other excuse for looking out the window. When she cranked that old car, all hell broke loose; and she came out of it in a dead run with her dress tail standing straight out. What a sight! The kids almost disrupted school, screaming and laughing.

After assembly that afternoon, she called me aside and said, "Dan, I know who put that bomb on my car, but I'm not mad at you. However, I would like to see you in my room after school."

I said, "Miss Donaldson, it's six miles from this school house to where I live, and I have walked it so many times that I know every rock in the road; then when I get home, I have lots of work to do. Whatever you feel like you need to do to me, you'll have to do it in a hurry, because I have to catch the bus."

As soon as the final bell rang that afternoon, I rushed to her room and got there before all the students had left. When the last one went out the door, she explained again that she most certainly was not mad at me. She said, "Dan, I have never whipped a student; and if you don't mind, I'd like to whip you."

I'm quite sure that she knew my rear end was as tough as a rawhide bottomed chair. I've wished many times that today's child abuse laws had been in effect when I was in high school. I'd have put Percy Foreman on retainer and the Colorado City school system would have belonged to me! I had been whipped that year with everything up to a one-by-four-inch board, so when she brought out a little stick that looked like it came off the side of an orange crate (which would not have hurt a five-year old), I was not exactly quivering in my boots, but she was as nervous as a pregnant fox in a forest fire. She repeated, "I've never whipped anyone before, so I may need a little advice."

I said, "I'm your man. I've had plenty of experience. First, I'm going to bend over and grab my ankles," which I did. Then I said, "OK, let 'er rip."

When she started to draw back the small board, I raised up and said, "No, no, no, use both hands, and lean on it. OK, I'm ready, let 'er go."

The smack she gave me would not have hurt a kindergarten child, but I jumped as high as I could and screamed like a banshee. Kids started running to the door, peeping through the glass to see who was dying inside. Miss Donaldson turned fourteen different colors and was unable to speak for a moment. When she finally could talk she said, "Dan, I guess you can go."

I raced out the door, turned the corner and literally laid down on the floor and laughed for a minute, then hurried out and caught the school bus.

Nearly 60 years have passed, and it's still as funny to me as it was that day. I'll never forget it, and I'll bet money she remembers the first spanking she ever dished out.

Chapter 14

Unusual Job Opportunities

I was only sixteen years old in 1943 when I graduated from high school at Colorado City, Texas. I thought I knew as much as anybody in the world and that I was 7 feet tall and bulletproof. I found several wonderful job opportunities during that first summer.

The first good job I found was with an oil company in South America for 2 years. A minor's release, signed by parents, was required for certain jobs, and the oil company job was one of them. When I casually mentioned to my mom and dad that I was going to South America, they laughed and said, "You must be crazy if you think for one moment that we would let you go to South America, and especially for two years." I really felt stepped on, but I lived over it.

Shortly after the South American opportunity, I found a really good job. It was in Odessa, Texas, driving a nitroglycerin truck, and paid $2.40 an hour. I figured that was more money than the President of the United States made, and I could hardly wait to go to work. When I brought this up at the supper table, my folks nearly fainted. It was probably the most dangerous job in the world, since nitro is awfully unpredictable and the most highly explosive product that we knew of at the time. I probably don't need to add that I did not get that job either. I had trouble understanding why the folks didn't realize that I was grown and should be able to do what I wanted to. Much later, as my own children became sixteen, I could understand it better.

The next foolish thing I did was caused by my desire to see the bright lights of Fort Worth, Texas. Dad had given me a small cotton crop as part of my pay for the summer, and I almost forced him to buy my crop in August of 1943. I took my few dollars and caught a cattle truck to Fort Worth. I figured I would make a million dollars pretty quickly. Sadly, that did not happen.

During the next few weeks, I spent more time hanging around the beer joints in Fort Worth than I did looking for a job. I had a number of menial tasks, which paid very little, so I certainly was dissatisfied. I was really looking for a white-collar job which paid well and didn't require much work. I had worked hard all my life and felt that with as much education as I had, I should find a job that would make me rich in a hurry. That did not happen either.

I was staying in the worst place in Fort Worth, I guess. It was an old rooming house where I slept in a large room with seven or eight other men. There was no air-conditioning and only a couple of windows which let in very little air. It was so hot and humid that many times, when I came in late at night, I would have to wet a bath towel and put it on my bed, so I could go to sleep. The only good thing about the room was that it didn't cost very much.

Paychecks had been pretty scarce for me in Fort Worth; so when I got up one morning, looked in my billfold, I found that I was about out of hamburger money. I had spent quite a bit of time at the Texas Employment Agency, so I had gotten pretty well acquainted with the manager. I went to see him, and explained that I was about broke.

I said, "I've been looking for a position; now I'm looking for a job. I've got to make some money so I can eat."

He told me, "There is a job at the Milwaukee Bottling Company, but I don't know how much it pays."

Thinking it must be a beer bottling company, I told him, "It doesn't matter what the pay is, I want that job!"

Early the next morning, I caught the bus out to the south part of Fort Worth where the Milwaukee Bottling Company was located. It turned out to be a soda pop bottling company, which certainly took some of the luster from the job!

The manager interviewed me at length, found out that I was raised on a farm and ranch, and asked me, "Do you know what hard work is?"

I told him, "Hard work is all I know!" So, he hired me at thirty cents an hour.

My first chore was to carry sacks of sugar up a stairway, which was almost straight up. The sacks weighed 100 pounds, and I weighed 130. I spent quite a while carrying sacks and was completely exhausted when I finished. I did some other jobs, but finally, I was sent to a large warehouse, where the only ventilation was one small window. It was the middle of August, so it was plenty hot and humid in that room.

There were four or five men shooting cases of pop bottles down a rolling ramp into the warehouse. My job was to sort the cases, and put them in the proper stacks. The only way I could keep up with my job was to go in a dead run. I did that for about an hour, but finally turned one of the cases over and sat down on it. In no time at all, the bottles backed up beyond the wall, through which they were coming into the warehouse.

One of the men from the outside stuck his head through the door and yelled, "White boy, you'd better get off your ass, and get to work!"

I grabbed a pop bottle in each hand and sent him back where he had come from.

I sat there for a few more minutes, and no one bothered me; but all of a sudden, I had all I wanted of that place. I got up, headed for the office and told the boss, "I'm quitting, and I'd like to get my check."

He said, "Aw hell, son, you haven't worked long enough for me to mess with writing a check. You've worked four hours, so you only have $1.20 cents coming, and that's not enough to fool with."

I said, "Mister, please pay me. It may not be much to you, but it's a lot to me."

He said, "Hell no, I'm not going to pay you."

Heatedly, I said, "Mister, I'm almost completely broke, and that's a lot of money to me. Would you please pay me?"

He answered, "Get the hell out of here boy! You're not getting any money from me!"

Finally, I said, "Mister, I've told you that I'm broke, and I need my money. You think $1.20 it not very much, but it will buy several hamburgers for me. I've asked you three times, as nice as I know how, to pay me; and you've refused. I don't have another job for today, so I guess I'll just spend the rest of the day around here, trying to whip your ass!"

He looked at me for a long time, and I looked him squarely in the eye. Finally, he reached into a desk drawer, pulled out a checkbook and paid me.

During that part of World War II, there was a provision whereby you were not supposed to change jobs unless you met certain requirements. They called it "freezing you to the job you were working on."

The man said, "You are frozen to this job, and I'll see that you don't get another one!"

"If there's not a better job than this, I hope to hell I never find another one!" I retorted.

The next day I heard that American Airlines was hiring; so I caught a bus out to Meachem Field, where American was headquartered. They were indeed hiring some people who would work for six months on probation, cleaning airplanes inside and out, etc. After the probationary period, I would be assigned to a better job. I don't recall what the pay was, it was not much, but after six months, I could work into a job with better pay; so I decided I could wait that long. They offered me the job, and I took It. They issued two khaki uniforms to me and told me to report for work the next morning.

I went back to my room, sat down on the bed and started thinking. This was the first time I had been gone from home for any length of time and I began to think about Colorado City. Suddenly,

I was overwhelmed with homesickness. I gathered up my few belongings, and took the two uniforms to the downtown ticket office of American Airlines. I told them I was not going to report for work the next day and asked them to return the uniforms to the office at Meacham Field.

September had rolled around by then, and I knew the cattle trucks from Colorado City would be coming into Fort Worth almost every night. I knew every bull hauler in Mitchell County; so I was pretty sure I could catch a ride home. I rode the bus out to the Fort Worth stockyards, and sat down to wait the night out. Sure enough, about 4:00 o'clock the next morning, five of my friends came in, each with a load of cattle. I told them I sure needed a ride home. Each one of them offered me a ride, but the only catch was, they were going to have to load five loads of prairie hay at Arlington that morning.

I said, "Man, I'll do anything for a ride home!"

It took us all day to load the hay by hand, and we finished up about sundown. We drove back as far as Weatherford, Texas; climbed up on top of a load of hay and slept until morning. We got back to Colorado City about the middle of the afternoon, and I hitched a ride out to my folk's house in the country. Boy, was I glad to get my feet under Mama's table again. I had been gone for about a month and had taken my belt up several notches.

It was quite awhile before I wanted to leave home again!

A couple of months later, I got a bill for $10.00 from American Airlines (addressed to Dad), to pay for the two uniforms. Evidently, someone had stolen them, so Dad mailed them a check, and I repaid him.

I've wondered, a few times, if I had stayed with American for these sixty some-odd years, if I might have worked my way up to Vice-President of Cleaning Airplanes.

Chapter 15

My Wife Joyce

During the fall of 1944, I went to the weekly Friday night dance at the Colorado City Country Club. I hadn't been there long until I spotted a girl that made my eyes pop out! She had long dark hair, green eyes and was as cute as a speckled pup. It didn't take long to find out that she was there with a friend of mine. The first time I had a chance, I asked her for a dance.

She was from Sweetwater, Texas, a town twenty-eight miles east. Her name was Wanda Joyce Walker. She was a beautiful girl with the sweetest disposition.... a real charmer! She was not as big as a minute......four feet, eleven inches tall, and weighed in at about ninety-eight pounds. I danced with her every chance I had and before the dance broke up, I asked her for a date for the next week-end and she accepted. I was out of my head at the thought of being with her. The date went well and we started going together on a regular basis.

World War II was going on and gasoline was rationed so I was unable to make the trip to Sweetwater as often as I wanted to.

Several months passed and I got a job in Sweetwater with Continental Oil Company, working on a seismograph crew, looking for oil. That surely worked well for Joyce and me to be able to see each other more often.

We were madly in love by that time and decided to get married on November 29, 1945.

We got some bad news about the middle of October. Continental was moving my crew to Plainview, Texas, one hundred sixty miles

Joyce Walker Fields at wedding reception on November 29, 1945.

away. I moved with them but went back to Sweetwater each weekend. It seemed like November 29th would never come, but finally it did.

The Rev. J. E. Shewbert married us in the old Highland Heights Methodist Church in Sweetwater. (That church was destroyed by a tornado many years later.) We were the happiest couple in the world, I know! After a brief honeymoon in San Angelo, Texas, we headed for Plainview where my crew was still located.

We had only been there for a few days when Joyce became violently ill and had to go to the hospital. I was absolutely scared to death!

Almost the same day, the seismograph crew was ordered to move to Artesia, New Mexico. After the crew moved to Artesia, I was left in a strange town with a bride that I was afraid might die. I didn't know what to do. The doctors were unable to determine Joyce's problem, so they started giving her large doses of penicillin, a new drug that had been discovered and was being used primarily on the service men during the war. In desperation I called her mother and she came up to help take care of her.

When she finally improved enough, her mother took her back to Sweetwater with her so that she could give her better care than I could, while I went on to join my crew at Artesia. I was only nineteen years old and was one worried and lonesome young man.

Joyce stayed with her mother until Christmas. During this time my crew had moved to Las Vegas, New Mexico and then on to Roswell, New Mexico. I joined Joyce for the holidays and when Christmas was over I finally got to take her back to Roswell with me. We rented a small, converted chicken house and were as happy as two pigs in the sun.

Continental kept us on the move for several months until we finally wound up in Spur, Texas. Our crew had lived in eleven towns during a ten month period. Packing and unpacking was fairly simple, as we had about three dynamite boxes full of our belongings, and as we moved into a place, Joyce would open the lid, take out a crocheted doily and a vase for the top of it, close it back and we were in business.

Joyce had still not been well, and during this time, she went to Sweetwater to see her family doctor. He said her appendix had ruptured in Plainview and the penicillin had saved her life. He operated on her and she was finally well and back with the crew again.

By this time, we had our fill of moving. I took a new job in Sweetwater as a clerk in Armors Drug Store, where I worked for a few months. It was not the kind of job that I liked and it paid nearly nothing but I stayed until Dad found a farm near his that I could rent. Joyce had been working at Western Windmill Company, but we were happy to move near my folks and start farming.

We took the place and went into debt for $2850.00 to buy an old tractor and an old milk cow and calf.

I think the happiest day of our lives was the day we moved to the country and started farming.

Chapter 16

Three Wrecks on the Same Horse

I remember that in the spring of 1943, the Spade Ranch, which was a big outfit south of us, sold some good yearling, paint, filly colts. I knew they raised good horses, so I bought one of them. A neighbor of ours, Herschel Cockrell, who was also the local John Deere tractor dealer, bought another one. I left home that summer, before my colt was old enough to break. I was gone several years during the war, and during that time, the colt died.

In the fall of 1946, my dad bought Herschel's filly. Dad told me she was "plenty of horse," but I couldn't imagine Herschel owning one that was worth a damn. Dad didn't know that Herschel had allowed her to develop some bad habits. Dad was sixty years old, but still much of a man. He began to work the kinks out of his new purchase in a "not too gentle way." That didn't go on very long until she bucked him off.

I had married and my wife and I lived in Sweetwater, Texas at the time; but one day while visiting the folks, my mother told me about a bucking incident. It worried her because she knew that Dad was too old to be banged around like that, but he still seemed like a young man to me. I couldn't keep from kidding him about letting a plug horse buck him off. He just grinned and said nothing.

Later he started the same horse across a long, narrow overhead bridge on Champion Creek, which was on one side of our pasture. When she refused to cross the bridge, he got off, took out his pocket knife and patiently cut a club nearly as big as his wrist, from the limb of a mesquite tree. He got back on; and when he began to work her over from one end to the other, she downed her head and busted his ass right in the middle of the hard road. A neighbor caught her up the road and brought her back to him. He rode her to the house, turned her out in the pasture, and told my mother, "She's 'throwed' me twice, and that's enough!"

When Mama told me about it, I said, "Pop, I believe you've developed a bad case of the round ass since I've been gone." Again, he smiled and said nothing.

By that time, I had rented a farm near dad's place for the following year, and when I teased him about getting bucked off, he laughingly said, "Well, you're such a hotshot cowboy, we'll see if you can ride her when you move back out to the country."

When my wife Joyce and I moved to the farm a couple of months later, Dad could hardly wait for us to get our belongings unloaded before he said, "Let's go ride that paint filly!"

I had not been on a horse for three or four years, so I was pretty rusty. I got on her and warmed her up in the corral for a few minutes. Dad opened the gate and said, "Lope her out about fifty yards and turn her around."

I rode her "out a ways," and when I barely touched her neck with the rein, she suddenly changed ends. I was completely surprised, and I'll bet my ass was eighteen inches from the saddle. I grabbed all the leather I could find and barely stayed on. Dad was laughing so hard that he lost his breath. He would have given anything he owned if the filly had turned out from under me.

She was a fine piece of horse flesh, and might have been the best one I ever rode. I used her for the next two or three years, but she just felt compelled to pitch now and then. She never threw me, but got close several times.

One cold winter morning, I saddled her up to see about some cattle. She had not been ridden very much that winter and was feeling her oats. I was in a bad humor that morning; so when she got a hump in her back, I reached up in her shoulders and spurred her as far back as I could reach. I thought she would buck, so I had sat down tight in the saddle. She never started to pitch, but suddenly folded up her hind legs, rolled backward, and barely missed pinning me with the saddle horn. She wound up on her right side with my right leg under her. I had lost the reins, and I was not sure I had got my right foot out of the stirrup; so when I had one chance to grab the cheek of the bridle, as she got up, I really took a firm hold. I had no intention of being dragged to death! My foot had cleared the stirrup, but my ankle and knee were hurting awfully bad. I thought something was broken, but it was only a bad sprain in both places. I was crippled up some and on crutches for two or three weeks. Lots of horses will rare up, but I never had never seen a horse pull a stunt like that.

Dad was in town the next day, at the cattle auction, and ran into a couple of young fellows who were riding some colts. They said they could ride the paint and get her smoothed out in a few days. Dad told them, "I don't think so, but if you want to try, come out to our place tomorrow."

They showed up the next day and were certain they were capable of handling things. They saddled her up; and, with me standing there telling them exactly what she was going to do, she came within an inch of getting on top of one of them. Dad said, "That's enough; we'll get rid of this horse before she kills somebody."

Jess Thomas, an old horse trading friend of ours, picked her up the next day; and I never heard of her again. I'd bet money though, I was not the last cowboy she rolled backward on!

Chapter 17

The Cold Jawed Filly

As I drove my car down the street one morning, I watched the temperature drop about ten degrees in three miles; and I was reminded of a similar day more than sixty years ago.

One of our big steers had been missing for several days when a neighbor told me he was in his pasture several miles south of our place. One Sunday morning I decided to go after him. I was saddling my horse when a friend of mine, Howard Bynum, drove up and asked what I was doing. I told him, and he offered to come along and help me drive the steer back home. He was certainly welcome since he was a good cowboy, and I didn't have to pay him. I told him to catch the roan filly that I had traded for a few days before.

It was a cold day in January, but we had warm coats and were comfortable enough. As we rode south, we discussed a bad storm that we knew was coming in; but we didn't think it was due until later that night.

I laughed and said, "Howard, let me tell you about the filly you are riding. I traded for her three or four days ago and have only ridden her once. The morning after I traded for her, I went out to the trap to drive her into the pen; but she was gone. Evidently she had jumped the fence during the night. I threw my saddle in the pickup and started down to the other place to catch another horse, but one of my neighbors stopped me and told where I could find her. I located her a couple of miles from home, hemmed her up in a corner and roped her. I didn't have a bridle with me, so I just threw a half hitch over her nose with the lariat rope, jumped on and started down the road toward home."

I continued, "She had seemed gentle enough and had handled well the day before, so I was not expecting any problems. As we jogged down the road toward home, however, she began to pick up speed. I tightened the rope on her nose, but she continued to run faster. When we came to a turn toward my house, there was a lot of gravel on the road; so I didn't try to turn her for fear she would fall. She was running full tilt, and it took me a long time to turn her around; but when we came back down the road, she had slowed down enough to make the turn toward home. She cut loose again, however, and ran another half a mile. Then when she started to slow down, I began to wear her ass out with my lariat rope. When I finally got her to the house and got a bridle on her, she had had all the running she wanted; so we both settled down and went on about working cattle."

Howard said, "Don't worry, I can handle this filly; and I don't give a damn if she runs or not!"

As we rode along, we caught each other up on the news; but we were keeping an eye on the northern horizon. We surely needed to finish up our work and get home before the storm hit. We knew the pasture where we were going, so it didn't take long to locate the steer, cut him out from the neighbor's cattle, and start him toward home, which was four or five miles away.

By then we had noticed a blue line across the northern sky, so we knew that the storm was approaching. We decided we would be lucky if we made it home before the bad weather hit.

Evidently the steer had made a lot of good friends in the pasture where he had been visiting because he sure as hell was not anxious to go home. We drove him to a county road and headed him north, but he took every wrong turn that he could find; and when there wasn't a road to turn into, he went through the fence. This was a slow process; and before we got halfway home, the wind had switched to the north. The temperature was falling like a turd in a cistern, and a light rain was coming down. Because of the way their hair grows, cattle don't like to travel into the wind. It became increasingly difficult to keep the steer between the fences.

We were almost frozen by that time. The rain had started to freeze on the fences and bushes, and we were getting wet. I was so cold that I was not thinking very well. It suddenly dawned on me that we were at the top of a long hill that ran down to a narrow, overhead span bridge, with two steel runners. The steer was halfway down the hill when I yelled, "Howard, I don't believe that damned steer will cross the bridge. I'd like to take him the other mile and a half to the house, but our pasture is on the left side of this road; so if he jumps the fence again we've got a fifty-fifty chance that he'll be on our place. Let's chouse him and see if he might cross the bridge!"

We came down the hill with our horses in a run, whooping like a tribe of Indians; and lo and behold, the steer ran out onto the bridge. I was in the lead and began to slow down as I approached the bridge, but I looked back and saw that Howard was coming "hell bent for leather."

I yelled, "Pull up; there's ice on the bridge."

However, the filly had the bit in her teeth; and instead of slowing down, it looked as if she had changed to a higher gear as she came by me. It was quite a sight as they flew by me. Howard had lost his hat, his hair was flying in the wind, and his coattail stood straight out.

I heard him holler, "Whoa, you son-of-a-bitch!"

He was white as a sheet, and I'm sure I was too, because both of us could see that there could be a terrible wreck on the icy bridge. If the horse fell, she and Howard could crash into the steel side of the bridge, or be thrown over the rail where there was a thirty foot drop.

The horse's and steer's hooves were slipping on the icy bridge, and suddenly the steer fell right in front of the horse. My heart stopped for a few beats as the horse ran completely over the steer, but miraculously kept her feet. By the time my heart started to beat again, horse and rider had gone flying off the end of the bridge and were going up the road in a dead run. When I saw him and the filly go off the end of the bridge, I got off my horse to retrieve his hat and began to laugh hysterically.

Howard finally got the filly turned around and rode back down to the bridge, asking me to bring his hat to him. The rain had increased and water was running down the back of his neck. Time passed and he was getting colder with more water running down his shirt collar; but every time I tried to get back on my horse, I couldn't mount up for laughing. Howard called me some pretty bad names before I was able to get his hat to him.

The rest of the trip on was uneventful. We penned the steer, warmed up, dried out, and over a hot cup of coffee, rehashed our experience. Howard argues until this day that I knew the horse which I gave him was cold jawed and would probably run away with him.

Chapter 18

High Flying Cowboy

In the late 1940s, my father and I formed a partnership that lasted until he retired many years later. I often wondered how it endured for so long, since we were both strong-willed and outspoken individuals. However, it was one of the best things that ever happened to me; and I believe Dad felt the same way, though we never discussed it.

We were farming and ranching on Champion Creek, south of Colorado City, Texas. We also bought and sold a good many cattle—always in the market for some livestock that would make us a few dollars.

Once we bought a string of heavy boned, good quality, horned Hereford cows with big (three hundred and fifty pound) calves at their sides. They had come out of the Pecos, Texas country, hadn't seen many people, and were pretty much on the wild side. We bought them through the Midland, Texas auction, where they had inadvertently been infected with pink eye. Because of this, we had to do quite a bit of eye doctoring for several days. The quickest and easiest way for us to do that was to separate the calves from the cows, herding them into a small "crowd- pen," where I pushed them into a corner and, one by one, grabbed them by the head and held them while Dad squirted medicine into their eyes. When we finished with the calves, we moved into the larger corral where the cows were held. From horseback, I roped each of them; and while the horse kept the rope tight, Dad went hand over hand down the rope and doctored the struggling cow.

One day, while we were hard at work on the calves, a new neighbor and his fifteen-year-old son Richard stopped by to see what we were doing. They had recently moved from Houston, and I imagine the only cows that Richard had ever seen were the ones he had spotted along the highway. They climbed onto the corral fence, watched for a couple of minutes; then Richard asked eagerly, "Do you need any help?" He was a big boy, so Dad looked him over, and said, "Sure, Son, come on in."

That was a mistake! Richard had seen too many western movies. Instead of asking me how to hold those wild calves, he caught them by the tail, the legs, around the neck or anywhere else he could get a hold. We tried to tell him what to do, but he wouldn't listen. He was having so much fun that we hated to order him out of the pen, so he continued his reckless behavior. Somehow we finished working the calves, in spite of Richard's assistance.

His dad had gone home when we moved to the larger corral and started to doctor the cows. This was work where a greenhorn youngster like him could get hurt, so I told him in no uncertain terms to get on the fence and stay out of our way. There was just too much excitement for him to do as he was told. Dad and I were too busy to keep an eye on him all the time, so he kept jumping off the fence to help us. His favorite place seemed to be between me, on horseback, and a big wild cow with a rope around her neck—not a healthy place if you failed to pay attention.

Finally, it happened—Richard got in the wrong place at the wrong time! I roped a cow that broke crosswise in front of me, putting a lot of slack in the rope. The big bay horse I was riding had his rear end against the fence and couldn't immediately back up to take the slack out of the rope. Richard was standing between the cow and me, scratching his behind, daydreaming, and staring in the wrong direction. When the stampeding cow hit the end of the lariat, the rope caught Richard from behind, in the bend of his knees, catapulting him at least six feet into the air. I couldn't tell whether he did two or three backward flips; but at one point he was level with me sitting on the big horse, looking straight up toward Jesus. He had a surprised look on his face and a wild look in his eyes, as though he wondered if heaven was near. However, he returned to earth, with a smack, hitting flat on his back on the hard, hoof-packed ground. The impact seemed to rattle the fence posts. Richard lay still. I rolled off my horse, unable to do anything but laugh. I looked at Dad, and like me, he was doubled over with laughter. By the time we were able to get to the would-be cowboy, his breath was returning, and he was coming around. His feelings were hurt because we laughed at him, but he was O.K. However he was through cowboying, and decided his mother was looking for him. We told him we would take him home when we finished our work, but he struck out on foot.

Richard lived near us for several years; but I guess he gave up working cattle, because he never offered to help us again.

Whenever Dad and I recalled this time, we always reacted the same way—with wild laughter. We agreed it was a situation in which if we had known Richard was lying dead in the middle of that corral, there was no way we could have gotten to him any sooner.

Chapter 19

El Toro Malo

Dad, N. O. Brown (our neighbor) and I, were at the cattle sale barn in San Angelo, Texas one day, and I bought a good Brahma bull. He seemed pretty gentle when he came through the auction ring, but when we ran him into the alley, getting ready to load him into a trailer, he was plenty salty. We worried around with him for ten or fifteen minutes; and in the meantime, I roped him. He finally jumped over a gate as high as my head, and hung the rope on the hinge of the gate causing him to hang himself, with his feet about four feet off the ground.

A Brahman bull

Dad was all in a dither and hollering at me to cut the rope or the bull would choke to death. I said, "I hope the son of a bitch does." I really didn't intend for him to choke himself, but I left him there for a couple of minutes, which took the fire out of him. When I let him down from the gate, he was ready to get into the trailer.

We stopped in Robert Lee, Texas for coffee, and the bull had revived somewhat by then. While we were drinking coffee, we could hear the bull, outside the restaurant, trying to kick the end gate out of the trailer.

N. O., or "Ought," as we called him, was a very good friend of mine. Ought and Dad were good friends, too, but for some reason Ought and I had a special bond that lasted until his death. He was a gentleman in every way, but he always saucered his coffee. When his coffee was served, he would pour about a third of it into his saucer, slurp loudly, and pour in another third. He would slurp loudly one more time, pour in the last slurp and say, "Hell, boy, drink that coffee, we've got to go."

The day in Robert Lee was no exception; Ought slurped his coffee and said, "Let's get out of here, before that damn bull tears up the trailer."

I replied, "There's no hurry, maybe the son of a bitch's foot will get sore."

When we got home with him, he was still raising hell. I thought he needed to settle down for a while, so I chained him to a big snubbing post in the middle of the corral, which I called the "calming post." I gave him just enough room to eat, drink, and lie down. I left him chained to the post for a week or ten days, which should have been more than ample time for him to gentle down. However, he just seemed to get worse; so one day I drove a bunch of cattle into the corral with him and turned him loose.

He was one mean mother! He charged my horse whenever I went near him in the pasture. That got old pretty fast, so finally I took a fourteen foot bull whip and knocked about three pounds of hair off him, which changed his attitude a bit. While he was in the pasture with some of the other cattle he was OK, but when we had to bring them down to the corral he was plenty bad.

One day my mother asked me if I would consider getting rid of him. She said, "Julius won't say anything to you about it, but he's afraid that bull is going to kill someone, and it could be you. We're afraid to keep him."

I was not particularly worried about the bull hurting me; but if it bothered my folks that much, then it was time for him to go. I located another bull that I thought would be satisfactory, bought him, brought him home and turned him out in the pasture.

The next day I got on my horse and Dad and I penned the bad bull (toro malo) three times, and each time he wrecked the corrals. I was damned sure tired of fixing fence by that time, so I told Dad, "Hook up the trailer, and I'll take care of this son of a bitch."

I remounted my horse, built a loop and tied on to the bull. He was a big one and a sure enough handful; but when Dad brought the trailer, I managed to drag him into it.

We hauled him to the auction barn at Colorado City, Texas, and he was raising plenty of hell when we drove up. The men who ran the barn came rushing out to tell me they were not having a sale the next day, and I would need to take this wild son of a bitch back home. I replied, "0h, no, this bull has seen all of the country south of here that he's ever going to see. You can board him until you do have a sale, and I don't give a damn if it's a month." They were not very happy with that answer.

When he finally sold, the following week, he had lost weight and looked like a gutted snow bird. However, he had almost wrecked the pens at the auction barn. Everyone who had walked by him during the week had thrown their hat under him just to see him tear down some more gates.

I don't know if the sale owners were madder at the bull for wrecking things or at me for bringing him to the sale.

Chapter 20

Seven Wells

For thousands of years, there was a wonderful place at the confluence of the North and South Champion Creeks, roughly six miles south of Colorado City, Texas, called Seven Wells for the number of natural springs located there. The area covered several acres of solid sandstone, where the two creeks had cut strange patterns through the rock in the canyons, making whirls and swirls in unbelievable designs. Many of the holes were perfectly round, three to ten feet wide. One was the shape of a twenty-foot skillet, while others were of odd shapes and various sizes. The depths varied from ankle deep to twenty-five or thirty feet. The springs flowed clear, cold water year round. I never saw them dry up, even in the worst years of drought.

In 2001, bones of a mammoth were recovered a little over two miles from Seven Wells, proving there had been life in the area for millions of years. Buffalo had come there to water for centuries, with large groups walking in single file, each stepping in the exact place where the one before had stepped, wearing holes six to eight inches deep in the sandstone where they had walked.

Where there were buffalo, there were Indians who had also congregated there for hundreds, maybe thousands of years. Then came the white man and they too stopped and drank the cold, clear water. First, the scouts and soldiers, then the wagon trains, later big cattle herds being driven north to Kansas, and finally the settlers.

Scouts and soldiers drove the Comanches, Apaches, and other tribes away, making it safe for the pioneers moving through the country in wagon trains. Those pioneers endured daily hardships, as evidenced by a tiny grave almost hidden in the heavy brush about a mile west of the springs. A small girl had been buried there in the 1880's. A grieving relative must have returned after her death, because a simple white headstone marked the grave, with her name and dates of birth and death. Sadly, I remember none of the names or dates. A low rock fence surrounded the grave, and I used to ride by there every year or so to replace the rocks knocked down by animals.

My friends and I came to the springs mostly to walk over the area and picture in our minds all the things that had taken place there. We walked in the carved out areas where the buffalo walked, and our imaginations came to life. We imagined the thousands of buffalo coming there for water. We spent hours watching the surrounding area for the Indians coming to hunt the buffalo—— or us. We could almost hear the sounds of the soldiers, wagons, horses, and the voices of the people in the wagon trains, stopping to camp, water their stock and bathe in the cool spring water. Seven Wells was not widely known, but it was a place enjoyed by folks from miles around who came there to picnic, swim, and fish, and by boys who carved their sweethearts' names in sandstone. I rode by there many times, stopped for a cool drink for my horse and me, and found a shady place to sit and meditate.

In 1960, a dam was built on Champion Creek, below Seven Wells, to provide water and electricity for a growing population, causing this wonderful historic place to be covered with water. For me, it was an incredible loss. I don't understand why the state allowed that to happen, but I guess that's progress.

Now, the only remains of this historic area are a few of the buffalo tracks which were sawed out of the sandstone and placed in a museum in Colorado City, Texas. In 2001, my friend Howard Bynum called me and said, "Dan, it's been so dry that Lake Champion has lowered enough to expose the old Seven Wells area. If you ever want to see it again, now is the time."

I drove there, and could see from the highway that mud had filled the creeks where the pristine springs had flowed, and silt had settled over the entire area. Weeds and brush covered the rocks where the tracks had been. Nothing was the same. A rich, historic site was now gone forever.

I could not bring myself to stop the car.

Chapter 21

Case of Mistaken Identity

George Poster was a small rancher in Mitchell County, Texas, and as ornery, contrary and sometimes as rude a person as you might know. I had known him most of my life, so I understood, and even liked the old bastard; but he was not a very lovable person.

George drove out to his ranch early every morning; and when he had completed his chores, he came back to Colorado City, and usually hung around the Pikes Peak Club. That was a private club for playing pool, cards, dominos, etc. George was playing "Shoot The Moon" in the Pikes Peak Club one day, when a nice looking, well dressed, young man came in and asked, "Where can I find Mr. Poster?" Someone pointed out George, and the stranger approached his table.

He said, "Mr. Poster, I'd like a word with you."

The old man said, "Have a seat over there, young feller, I'll get around to you after a while."

Mr. Poster finished the game he was playing and started another. The young man went to his table again and said, "Mr. Poster, I want a word with you right now. I'm with the Federal Bureau of Investigation!" The old man turned white as a sheet, and his mouth flew open wide enough to throw a tom cat in it.

The FBI man said, "Mr. Poster, I am looking for a Mexican from California on a charge of illegal flight to avoid prosecution. Some of his relatives work for you, and there's a possibility that he could be at your ranch." As he finished explaining his business, he handed his I.D. card to Mr. Poster.

The room was not well lighted, and George's vision was not 20-20; so he squinted as he peered at the identification card and said,

"Yep, yep, that's him all right. Mean looking son of a bitch."

The agent said, "No, Mr. Poster, that's my picture."

George never saw the humor in that incident, so it was never safe to mention it to him, as long as he lived.

Chapter 22

Dry Weather Country

A West Texas rancher was trying to sell his Culberson County ranch to a fellow from "up north." Culberson County, located in far West Texas, is one of the most arid areas in the state.

He had shown the ranch to the prospective buyer, who seemed quite interested. He had also learned that the northerner hated snow and was definitely not going to buy anything where he might have to contend with snow again.

Knowing it was possible that this good prospect might return to the ranch, alone, for another look, and to ask questions of Juan, his wetback Mexican cowboy, he said, "Juan, if the Yanqui comes back out here, you tell him this is a good ranch; and it doesn't snow here."

"Si, Senor," was the reply.

A few days later the buyer suddenly lost all interest in the ranch and would hardly talk to the owner. Wondering what might have happened, the rancher asked the cowboy if he had seen the Yankee. Juan was not a Rhodes Scholar, and his English was not the best.

He replied, "Si, he be comin' here."

"What did you tell him?" asked the rancher.

"I tell heem es rancho muy bueno."

"Did you tell him it doesn't snow here?"

"Si, Senor, I tell heem"—I say, 'I be here three yearse, never snow, rain two time'."

Chapter 23

The Big One That Didn't Get Away

Howard Bynum and I have been friends for 70 years, having met when we were small boys in school at Seven Wells, a two-teacher school south of Colorado City, Texas. Fishing was our favorite past time and through the years we have spent many happy days 'wetting the hook'.

In the late 1940s and early 1950s (before Lake Amistad was built), Howard and I fished the Rio Grande river on the Mexican border above Langtry, Texas. We went twice a year, once in March and again in October, when the weather was not quite so hot in that part of the country. We couldn't afford a boat, so we swam the river, which was wide and swift. As good swimmers, we had no problem with that. We fished both the Mexican and American sides, using throw lines. That was a heavy line tied to a tree with hooks and a heavy weight tied on the other end, which we threw out into the river, and that's why we called it a 'throw line'. We used gold fish for bait, and took turns swimming the river with the gold fish in a canvas minnow bucket with the handle held tightly in our teeth.

While we were there in March of 1951, a Blue Norther was whistling in. It was cold as the dickens and since we were swimming the river, the cold was almost unbearable. The next morning we crossed to the Mexican side and found that we had caught a big yellow catfish, which was the biggest one we had ever caught. We couldn't imagine how we were going to get him back across the river without him drowning both of us, since he was awfully strong in the water. We remembered we had a long, strong line in the pickup truck, back on the American side up on top of the bluff. We went after the line and did some figuring.

We estimated the river was probably about 40 feet at the deepest point, so we tied the catfish far enough from the end of the line that he could not pull either of us under if he went to the bottom of the river. I swam across to the American side with the long end of the line, while Howard hung on to the other end. We knew that if the fish went down 40 feet, we would both still be above water. We kept the line as tight as a fiddle string and the fish couldn't move very much. He thrashed around some, but I really believe we could have brought a hundred pounder across. By the time we got him to the American side, we were nearly frozen.

Dan, smiling, as he proudly holds the forty-five pound catfish he and Howard Bynum caught on the Rio Grande.

He was the only fish we had caught on the trip, so we talked it over and decided to go home. It was just too cold to stay down there on that river.

We loaded up and started out, got nearly to Comstock and I said, "Let's stop here and weigh that fish."

Howard said, "No, let's take him on up the road a little further. He won't look so big to people down here, but up close to home, he'll look like a big son-of-a-gun."

That's what we did. We hauled him about 300 miles to Robert Lee, Texas, which wasn't too far from home.

We stopped and weighed him on some platform scales at a grocery store. Word quickly got around about the 'big fish' in town, and everybody in Coke County came down to the store to see it.

He weighed 45 pounds. That was the biggest fish we had every caught. Everybody wanted to know where we caught him. We told them we caught him about 5 miles south of Robert Lee in the Colorado river with a cane pole and a grasshopper for bait.

As we drove out of town, Howard and I laughed hysterically, as we figured everybody in town would be down on the river the next morning with a cane pole and a sack full of grasshoppers.

PART III

Fifties Pioneers At Higginbotham, Texas

Chapter 24

Movin' West

My family was more or less pushed out of Mitchell County, Texas by the drought of the 1950s.

My Dad and I were farming quite a bit of land (about 3 sections) south of Colorado City, Texas. We were also running cattle, trading cows and doing custom work for the public, which involved combining and building terraces.

We planted some of our land in Milo and some in Sudan (a sweet sorghum) for forage for the cattle. Things were going pretty well for us, but in 1951 a drought had started and the feed dried up.

We also had about 750 acres of cotton planted and it only made 44 bales that year.

The only grass we had was along the banks of Champion Creek. We had always allowed people to fish and seine minnows in the

Dan building terraces in Mitchell County in the late 1940's

creek; but they scared the cattle away from the grass, so we finally posted our land.

The drought continued and by late that summer we were most discouraged.

Tom Hargrove, my brother-in-law, and his brothers had located some land in Gaines County, Texas, on the New Mexico state line. It was still prairie land and uncultivated. It was part of the Higginbotham Ranch that they were selling; and it had an ocean of water under it, which could be used for irrigating our crops. They told Dad and me they would buy 200 acres of the land and build a house for each of us, if we would move up there and farm it.

Howard Bynum, Julius, and Albert branding south of Colorado City, Texas

My dad, mother, Joyce and I talked about the move for a long time and on several occasions. Dad and Joyce were "rarin' to go," while Mama and I had reservations about it. I was partial to the cattle business while Dad enjoyed the farming part more.

Joyce was probably more excited about the prospect of a new house. She was a city girl and an only, pampered child. Living in the country was a real culture shock for her. I don't know why in the world she stayed with me, but I'm sure glad she did. We were currently living in an old house with uneven floors, no closets, no running water, and no plumbing. We had an old two-holer outhouse, but we had to crawl through a barbed wire fence to get to it, which was a real problem if you were in a hurry.

Joyce was, and is, about the most creative person I have ever known. We had two little baby girls with lots of frilly dresses, but no closets. Joyce used apple crates, making two stacks about four feet high, to make shelves. She put a pipe across the top and that was a rod for the dresses. Ruffled chintz material was used for a curtain across the front and, "Wow!"—a closet! To make a closet for her and me, she just stacked the apple crates higher and made the curtain out of a bedspread. Of course, the curtain had to match the spread for our bed and the curtains on the windows.

We hauled our drinking water in barrels from Dad's place since our windmill water had too much gypsum in it to drink. Since we had no water piped into the house, we carried huge water cans from the windmill into the kitchen. Of course, Joyce dressed them up, with a chintz curtain around them. Any water for cleaning and bathing had to be heated on the old cook stove. It was also hard to carry every drop of water and garbage out of the house, including the dish water, mop water, and of course the bath water, which was in No. 3 washtubs. The worst part was washing all those cloth diapers. Yuk!! I finally piped cold water from the windmill to the kitchen to use for cleaning and bathing. Joyce thought we were really making progress!

We cooked and heated the house with butane, but the tank froze every time it got very cold. When that happened, Joyce and the kids stayed in bed until I got the heat going. I had to build a fire outside and heat water which I poured over the regulator on the tank, to thaw it out. Once or twice I got so damned mad, I threatened to build a fire under the tank to build up enough pressure to blow the ice out of it! I probably would have blown up the house and the whole family, if I had tried that.

Joyce still managed to entertain her Study Club, our bridge club and church groups with dinners and parties. It was an all week preparation for her, but people seemed to enjoy it. They kept coming back, even though we had to run the chickens off the front porch a few times to let them in.

I think as mad as I ever saw her was when she had carried water from the windmill in a bucket to water some bulbs which she had set out in the hard packed dirt around the house in an attempt to grow flowers. It had been so much work; and one day she discovered the neighbor's hogs rooting up the bulbs and eating them.

After taking all things into consideration, we finally made the decision, as many pioneers before us had done, to move out to the unknown and unsettled west.

We loaded up and shipped all of our cattle, a couple of hundred head, to Fort Worth, Texas. I rode the truck with the last load of odds and ends about the first of December, 1951. Two big jobs for Dad and me were selling equipment that we wouldn't need in Gaines County, and getting everything else ready to move.

One day I was complaining to my friend Ought Brown about leaving all my good neighbors.

Ought said, "Let me tell you a story: I had a friend who was moving out of the country with his family. They had their belongings loaded in a wagon and stopped by my place to tell me goodbye. He told me, 'It just makes me sick to move off and leave my good neighbors. They are the best people in the world and will do anything for you.' I told him he'd find them that way where he was going.

A short time later another neighbor stopped to visit. He was also moving out of the community and said, 'I'll be so glad to get away from these neighbors. They're the sorriest people in the world, and I don't have any use for any of them. They're a no good bunch of folks.' I told him he'd find them the same way where he was going."

Ought finished his story by saying, "Dan, you will find good neighbors wherever you go."

He was right, of course. But as we prepared to leave everything and everyone we had known for so long, it was both an exciting and nerve-wracking time.

Chapter 25

Settling the Prairie

During the fall of 1951, the Hargrove boys, Dad and I made several trips to the new farm in Gaines County, checking on the many things that were going on. We cooked our meals on an open fire and slept under the stars in our bed rolls.

We lined up Caterpillar tractors and other heavy equipment, labor crews, plus a jillion other details prior to moving. The land was plowed with a back end plow on a big Caterpillar tractor to rip out the scrub mesquite. It plowed up the roots and stumps under the mesquite trees which were a lot larger than the tree itself. The crews then gathered up the stumps and brush, put them in piles and burned them. The weather was dry and the ground so hard in places the plow tore out clods as big as a refrigerator. That certainly caused us some problems when we started to prepare the ground for a crop.

We had two irrigation wells drilled, each one about a hundred and twenty feet deep, but the water rose in them to sixty or seventy feet, which is what the lift actually was. We installed ten inch diameter turbine pumps in them, and with enough horsepower they would put out 2,000 gallons a minute. (That would have amounted to more than $10,000.00 per minute, if we could have sold it for a dollar a bottle as they do now.)

Let me relate a couple of humorous things that happened during this time. We always stopped in Seminole, Texas to buy groceries. The Hargroves were all big eaters, and so were Dad and I; so there was always lots of food. Among other things, we always had some "Our Darling" brand canned corn. The Hargrove boys called it "Ar

Darlin'." It was the best corn I ever ate, but it's been off the market for a long time. When time came to open the cans of corn and other vegetables, Tom and his brothers always asked, "Who's got a pocket knife?" There never was a Hargrove who owned a good knife, so it seemed that nobody except me ever had one. I always carried a sharp, two bladed, Case knife; and I was very careful about what I used it for. They always got around to saying, "Dan, I know you've got one."

"That's right," was my answer, "but you're damn sure not going to open a can with it!"

"Aw, come on, it won't hurt it."

My reply was, "I know it won't hurt it because you're not going to use it." They usually wound up knocking a hole in the end of the can with a tire tool.

We worked hard on those trips, but managed to have a little fun, too.

When we bought the two new houses and moved them in from Lubbock, Texas, it proved to be a challenge. The road ended about a mile from our place and the trucks had to take the houses down a cow trail to the location on our place. We were so proud of them! Each of them had four rooms and a bath. We set them about fifty yards apart, facing each other, with a circle drive between. Later, we set out trees and planted White Dutch Clover in the circle.

Before Thanksgiving, Tom, Joyce and I went up there and fixed both houses. They were new, but they were not finished or painted inside. We filled and stripped the cracks in the sheetrock, hung wallpaper on some of the walls, and textoned and painted the others. We had no electricity, so we had no plumbing or water, and we cooked on a butane hotplate. We had to clean our paint brushes and everything else at an irrigation well a half a mile away. We slept on cots and had kerosene lamps for light; so when sundown came, we had to quit working. It was slow going, but we worked from sun up 'til sundown. Danna and Debby had stayed with Mom and Dad at Colorado City. On Thanksgiving Day, Rex and Sibyl, my sister, Bargy (Tom's wife), Mom and Dad and the girls brought Thanksgiving dinner and spent the day with us. What a meal, after eating warmed up grub for a week!

We were exhausted when we finally finished both houses after only two weeks. We were happy to get back to Colorado City and the girls.

Next, several of us men went up, camped out again, and plumbed the houses. We had moved a two room house for our farm hands nearby, but they were responsible for making it livable. We hooked up butane tanks, so we had heat but no electricity. The electric line ran past our house, but the electric company said they would have to wait a while to turn on our power. It turned out to be much later, about six months!

Finally we were through with our houses! When I returned home that time, we did as many pioneers before us had done—we loaded our equipment and all our worldly goods on every truck and trailer we owned and struck out for the unknown and unsettled west.

One of the funniest things I witnessed during the move, was when one of our hands named Geronimo Perez pulled out from our place south of Colorado City in an old jeep with a rocking chair tied to the top, the back end piled as high as it could be with odds and

One of the two identical houses moved onto the Higginbotham Ranch land that had been sold for cultivation.

ends, a #3 three tub tied to the top of that, and a border collie dog sitting on the seat beside him. I laughed at the sight until he turned the corner a mile up the road.

There was also another interesting incident involving two of our hands, Geronimo and his brother Tomas. It was a distance of about a hundred and sixty-five miles from where we lived south of Colorado City to Higginbotham, Texas, our new home. Geronimo, Tomas and I drove three tractors, towing equipment because it saved a lot of money. I drove our huge I-9 International tractor, towing a Hancock elevating terracing machine through Big Spring, Texas, and on northwest to the High Plains.

Geronimo and Tomas took a different route through Snyder, Texas, each driving a Model A John Deere tractor; one pulling a combine and the other towing a big trailer loaded heavily with equipment of various kinds. They left our place, south of Colorado City, before daylight. Dad and Mama had spent the night in Snyder with my brother Rex and his wife, Sibyl; so Dad had told the boys to meet him at a truck stop in Snyder at 8:00 o'clock that morning.

About a mile before the boys got to the truck stop, they approached a narrow bridge on the two lane highway. Tomas was in the lead towing a combine; and as he pulled off the highway to wait for approaching traffic to pass, he failed to leave Geronimo enough clearance to get his tractor and trailer completely off the highway. At the same time, a little snub-nosed milk truck approaching them from the rear, drove into the back of Geronimo's heavily loaded trailer. He tore up the truck and broke all the milk he was carrying, but didn't hurt Geronimo's trailer. Geronimo and Tomas knew Dad was waiting for them, and they didn't know what to do; so they looked around a little bit and hauled ass. Dad and Rex met them at the truck stop and were told what had happened. Since the boys had already left the scene of the accident, Dad told them to go on toward Higginbotham; and if the cops needed them, he would come to get them. The police were not too happy about the Mexicans leaving the scene but decided not to pursue them.

Dad, the two boys and I met at the farm at Higginbotham later that afternoon. Geronimo hated like the dickens to tell me what had happened; but the way he told it, all I could do was laugh.

He said, "I see thees leetle trok acomin', acomin'!" He was making all kinds of gestures in order to show me what had happened.

He added, "I theenk he no gotee some brakes."

Dad had turned the accident problem over to Rex to settle with the insurance company. Later, when Rex was dealing with the insurance adjuster, who represented the milk company, he told him we had a witness who said he thought the milk truck had no brakes. The adjuster laughingly confessed to Rex that the driver was afraid to apply his brakes for fear of breaking the milk in his truck; however, he broke the milk and tore up the truck, too! The adjuster told Rex that we might as well forget the whole thing.

I made several trips, moving most of the equipment on trailers or by truck. We still had one saddle horse named Chico, a couple of milk cows and some equipment to move.

We moved Mom and Dad to Gaines County before Christmas of 1951, and Joyce and the girls stayed to help them straighten up things, while I went back to Colorado City for another load of equipment. Before I could get loaded, an ice storm hit. We had no telephones, so I was worried about Joyce, the girls, and Mom and Dad; and I knew they were concerned about me. They had no way of knowing why I had not returned.

The ice finally began to melt after about a week, so one day after lunch, our hands and I hurriedly loaded a big trailer with some equipment. We got it loaded about sundown, and foolishly, I pulled out for Gaines County without a tail light on the trailer. I figured I might get caught by a highway patrolman but decided to take the chance.

About ten miles west of Snyder, Texas, I came over a hill and saw about six cars of highway patrolmen and sheriff's officers. I was sure one of them would stop me, but they didn't seem to pay any attention to me. I had gone three or four miles and decided that I was free and clear when I looked back and saw red and blue lights flashing. However, the patrol car blew by me without stopping. A little while later, I began to see where someone had thrown out cases of beer on the opposite side of the road. They were scattered about a half a mile apart. Every time I thought about stopping to pick up one, another patrol car went by. I finally figured out that the only reason the police were there was to keep someone like me from helping them pick up the beer.

I learned the next day that the police had jumped one of Pinkie Roden's bootleggers east of Lamesa, Texas and chased him to Gail. He had led the police on a merry chase all around Gail, throwing out cases of beer all the way. Pinkie's drivers always had the fastest cars that could be built; so when he finally got his car lightened up enough, he drove off and left the police.

We still had equipment back at the farm in Mitchell County that we didn't need on the plains, so Joyce, the girls and I stayed in Colorado City to finish up everything. We didn't say "Goodbye" to our old home until January 20, 1952.

It didn't take but a few weeks after we finished moving into our new home at Higginbotham for us to get tired of driving over the cow trail to reach our house. So when the county commissioner came by and said they were planning to build a road past our house, I volunteered to help him. We built a good dirt road in one day.

We began to meet neighbors who had just moved into the community to break out the new, raw land. We all came from different places, so everyone was eager to get acquainted. Our nearest neighbors were a half mile away: the settlement itself covered eight to ten square miles.

Some of those families were: Jack Thetford, Al and Jo White, Glen and Violet Upshaw, Bernice and Betty Hargrove, Preston and Genevieve Underhill, two families of Chadwicks, Albert and Billie White, her folks, Bill and Lois Looney, her aunt and uncle, the Cleve Looneys, and cousins Wanda and Max Kimbell. Two families that moved onto land already in cultivation were: James and Louise Crittenden and Horace and Joyce Hancock.

Some people who had lived in the community for a couple of years before we moved there were: LeRoy and Jean McGehee, the Melvin Hills, Frank and Mabel Freeman, their daughter Frankie Young, and their son W.D. (Dee) Freeman and wife Earlene, Bill and Joan Green, Lloyd and Nannie Mae Coats, Ancil Coats and wife, Eunice Crow (Louise Crittenden's mother), Roy and Nona Smith, and his brother O.B. Smith and wife, Verlon and Pauline Hilburn, Henry Payton and wife, Zack Payton and Barbara, Joe and Johnnie Woosley, and D.A. and Maudie Crowder, whose land we eventually bought.

Forrest and Azalea Freeman opened a general store in "downtown Higginbotham," in early 1952. They had one of the three telephones in the community and were wonderful about delivering messages all over the area. The other two phones were at the Paymaster Gin and the Lloyd Coats Butane Company. These phones were the type which were attached to a box on the wall with the ear piece hanging on the side. They also had a crank on the other side which you turned several times to ring an operator in Midland (about 120 miles away) who then put the call through to your party. By the middle of that year, the "city" boasted of a cotton gin, a general store, a blacksmith shop, and a cafe, all about five miles from our place. I thought at this rate, our population would surely catch up with Dallas, Texas in a few years!

More than fifty years have passed and my prediction is still 1,188,567 people short of reaching that lofty goal!

Chapter 26

It Wasn't As Easy As It Sounded

When we started farming the land in Gaines County, the first thing we had to do was to go over it several times with a big disk plow to break up the huge clods of dirt that the back end plow had pulled out. After we had finished that job; we pulled a land plane over it several times which leveled the ground considerably. When it was fairly smooth, we started listing, or making furrows in the soil. Dad kept busy running errands, hauling hands, etc.

That was during the drought of the 1950's, and no one can imagine the terrible sandstorms that came during the next two or three years. Every time we got a patch listed, the wind would get up and fill the furrows with sand. We did that over and over.

The real work began, however, when we started irrigating. We knew nothing at all about irrigation, or even how to survey the ditches. We didn't have the proper equipment to cut ditches and wouldn't have known how to use it if we had, but somehow or other we struggled through it. Every eight to sixteen rows, we built borders, which were higher than the furrows, and thus were able to force the water over the uneven ground. All of this was a real man-killer, but we managed to get it done.

There was another problem however, warm weather and irrigation water were flushing rattlesnakes out of their dens. We worried constantly about the girls because of the snakes being so numerous. They played outside much of the time since there was plenty of sand and water. I once killed six baby rattlesnakes, no more than seven inches long, in the yard. They were unable to rattle, but certainly were able to bite. There is no telling how many hundreds of snakes were killed on the several sections of new land which were being put into cultivation by us and our neighbors.

Several of the families usually got together once or twice a week for pot luck suppers and home made ice cream. The kids took turns sitting on the freezer, to hold it down while someone turned the crank. We used any excuse for a party—birthdays, anniversaries, or any other reason we could think of. During those get-togethers, the subject of rattlesnakes always came up. One neighbor might say his crew killed three snakes that week, another four or five, and occasionally someone killed more than that. Thank Goodness, after the first year the snake population diminished.

Needless to say, we felt like the true pioneers that we were. These were difficult but happy and exciting times. We didn't have much money, and I worked from daylight 'til dark, seven days a week, but we did take time out for church and Sunday school.

We used kerosene lamps for light in the house and knew we were moving up in this world when we were able to buy Aladdin Lamps, which made a brighter light. Joyce was the one who really had it rough, especially before we had electricity. She had the two little ones to see after, making all their clothes, her own, and some of my shirts, on an old pedal type Singer sewing machine. She went to town to wash and hung the clothes outside on a clothes line. She ironed miles of ruffled dresses and all the other clothes with a "sad iron," heated on the butane stove. Her arm would be red to her elbow when she finished ironing. It was hard to take, looking at the electric iron and the refrigerator, with no electricity to use them.

We hauled water in big barrels, which we kept by the back kitchen door. We were a happy bunch when we came home from town with blocks of ice, which we wrapped in quilts and kept in a wooden box outside.

One day I went by the house for a coke and found that the ice had melted. I had heard that you could cool a can of beer with liquid butane, so I decided to try that on the cokes. I put the bottles in a bucket and turned butane on them. "Boom!" They exploded (due to the rapid change of temperature), blowing glass all over that part of the county. Miraculously, no one was injured. In the meantime, the girls were growing and having a big time in our new home. They loved the freedom of running back and forth from our house to that of their grandparents, which was about fifty yards away; and of course, the folks enjoyed that too.

We started planting cotton in early May, and it was another struggle to try to get the crop up and going without the sand burning it off. We had to replant some of the cotton, but finally got all of it up.

Now, our thoughts turned to a more serious problem at home. Danna had been sick most of her life, with tonsillitis; and when she was three, before we left Colorado City, the doctors there had tried to remove her tonsils. Each time they attempted to remove one, she stopped breathing, so they halted the operation. They advised us to wait until she was at least four years old and stronger, and recommended that a specialist do the surgery.

About the last of May, we took her to Scott and White Hospital in Temple, Texas, where they removed her tonsils. We were glad we were in one of the best hospitals in the country, because she had a very serious problem. We were scared to death when she started hemorrhaging and they rushed her back into surgery to stop the bleeding. Thank Goodness, that was successful and she recovered in a few days. Joyce's mother Edith was with us; so when Danna was released from the hospital, we went to Oenaville, near Temple, and stayed a day or two with Edith's mother-in-law, Mrs. Barnwell, until Danna was able to go home.

We had two reasons to be thankful and happy when we returned home in June: Danna was okay, and the electric company had turned on the power to our house.

When the cotton was big enough, we ran a cultivator over it to plow furrows between the cotton rows, so we could run irrigation water down them. Before long we had a beautiful crop growing and were really proud of it. Fall came, and it looked as if we had a bumper crop, but unknown to us, cotton does not mature on sod land as quickly as it should. We had a very early freeze on October 7th which nearly ruined our crop. That made for a very disappointing year. However, since we had ample labor and equipment, during the year we had been able to get our crop in earlier than our neighbors. Consequently, our crop was considerably better than most of the others.

The year of 1953 was very much like 1952, except it was drier. The wind and sand were worse than the year before. Once that spring the wind blew fifty or sixty miles an hour, constantly, for seventy-two hours. During one storm, we were "riding it out" at a neighbor's house; and the sand came in so badly that the children were grading roads in the sand on the floor with toy graders. We covered everything in the house with sheets, but while we were eating, we got a lot of "sand in our craw."

At times, visibility was reduced to zero, driving into these storms was always dangerous. The sand literally sandblasted the paint and chrome off the front of the cars, and pitted the glass, sometimes to the point that it had to be replaced. Anyone who has not experienced a sandstorm like that could not begin to imagine what it is like.

A duststorm approaches our neighbor Bill Green's home, covering our land with strong winds, whirling sand and grit everywhere.

Chapter 27

The Bracero Days

During the 1950s and 60s, the United States government had an agreement with Mexico called the "Bracero Program" whereby Mexican nationals were able to come to work in the United States for a specified time at a guaranteed rate of pay.

In 1953 Dad and I were farming in Gaines County, Texas and had a beautiful cotton crop, but when it was ready to harvest, there were not enough native Americans available to pick the cotton, so we realized we needed to take advantage of that program.

The employer was required to furnish housing, bedding, cooking utensils, sacks for picking cotton and anything else they might need, because all they brought with them was their hat and their ass. These requirements were an awful lot of trouble and expense, but after talking over our options, Dad and I decided to go ahead and contract fifty braceros.

We built a barracks type building with bunk beds, a kitchen, for their living quarters, and outhouses. We bought all the required provisions so we would be ready for the pickers as soon as we could get the paper work done to legally process them.

I took the necessary documents to Eagle Pass, Texas, some four hundred miles away, down on the border of Mexico. I went in an open top truck so I could bring the braceros back home to Higginbotham.

We got home in the middle of the night and for miles, I had noticed lots of water in the ditches, so I knew we had gotten a big rain while I was gone. When I turned off the highway toward home, the cotton which showed in the edge of the dim truck lights looked strange. I couldn't figure out what was wrong. Suddenly,

I realized that cotton was strewn from the top of the stalk to the bottom, so I knew we must have had a big hail storm along with the rain.

I unloaded the men at the barracks, passed out their equipment and went home to sleep for a while. I was almost ill, but really didn't know how bad the crop was damaged until daylight. It was one big mess. The hail had knocked half of the cotton out on the ground and strung the rest up and down the stalk. Much of it was already stuck in the mud, and the rain kept falling for several days.

The Mexicans were unhappy because it was too wet to work, and they were so crowded in their quarters that they almost had to get out of bed one at the time. They were not nearly as unhappy as I was, because I could see a beautiful cotton crop practically destroyed and I had to pay them subsistence for the days they couldn't work.

Dan holding David at Higginbotham in 1953.

The first thing we did was to take them to the grocery store in Denver City, Texas to buy groceries, a chore which we had to do weekly.

Payday meant another weekly trip to the bank for cash. Then, Joyce, with the help of Chavelo our jefe (foreman), would set up a card table in the door of the pump house, where she handed out money to each bracero as he came by in line. I was always busy at the gin, so Joyce was alone with the braceros and all that money. We never even thought about that being dangerous because they were a good bunch of men, and besides, Chavelo would have protected Joyce with his life.

But I digress. After I got home from Eagle Pass with the workers, I realized that Joyce was due to have our third child any day. Before the weather cleared, she and I decided to make a quick trip to Brownfield, Texas to see our banker. As we drove along I said, "Joyce, I'm going to be mighty busy when the weather clears, so you would be doing me a big favor if you would go to the hospital tonight and have the baby."

She did! Our only son was born on October 24, 1953. He was a healthy baby and we named him Robert David. Danna and Debby, our two girls, were ecstatic over their new baby brother. He had the dark eyes, complexion and hair like his mother......and he was as cute as the girls.

When the weather finally cleared, we started gathering what little of our crop was left. It was a real mess! The braceros pulled the

Danna and Debby Fields watch as three braceros weigh a long sack filled with cotton on field scales. The braceros manually filled the sacks with cotton as they harvested the crop row by row. When the sacks were full, they weighed them and emptied them into trailers. The trailers were then towed to the gin.

cotton that was left on the stalk and dug some of it out of the mud, so we salvaged part of it.

We were more fortunate than our neighbors to the east who lost nearly everything. Some of them drug section harrows over their fields, then had their hands pick up the dirty stuff. Naturally, the quality of all our cotton was terrible.

However, we survived one more bad year, realizing that "that's the way farming goes . . . " and hoping for a better crop next year.

Chapter 28

The Lost Braceros

The government's Bracero Program worked well for us. The men we contracted were hard workers and were a very well-behaved group.

My dad was helping me around the farm after he retired, running errands, hauling hands, and whatever else needed to be seen after, while I worked at the gin. Dad did not care much for Mexicans, because of a problem with communication. He could not understand or speak one word of Spanish. However, when I asked him to, he hauled the braceros to town to get groceries, medical attention, or anything else they needed.

He drove up to the gin one day, madder than a wet hen—came rushing into the office, and said, "I just want to know what my job is!"

"What are you talking about?" I asked.

"Do I have to haul a bunch of these damned Mexicans everywhere I go? Every time I look outside, there's four or five of them sitting in the back of my pickup. I can't go to the mailbox or the neighbor's house or anywhere else without a bunch of those son-of-a-bitch's riding in the back of my pickup!"

I looked out the door, and sure enough, there were six of them perched in the back of his pickup. I said, "You don't have to haul them anywhere unless I ask you to. Get a stick and chase them out when you don't want to mess with them."

He said, "I'll damned sure do just that!"

I had about forty braceros that year, and two of them decided to go home before the season was over. I told my dad to pick them up and bring them by the gin so I could pay them before they left for

Mexico. Then, he would need to return them to the Lamesa, Texas office, from which they were contracted.

I had left the gin office and gone out to the local cafe to drink coffee, when Dad came along. He brought the two hombres inside, and I paid them. He mentioned that Mama was going with him to keep him company. I followed them outside, and as they drove off, I noticed there were two extra Mexicans in the back of the pickup. I called to them in Spanish as they drove away, and asked if they were going home, too.

They hollered back, "No, we're just going along for the ride."

Several days later, when payday came around, two men were missing. I asked the other fellows if they knew where they were.

They replied, "Sí, they went to Lamesa with your Papa."

It took me a few days to sort out what had happened. When Dad and Mama got to the contractors office in Lamesa, they took the two braceros who were going home inside and checked them in. Neither Dad nor Mama realized that two extra Mexicans had come along with them; so when they returned to the pickup and saw two hombres sitting in the back, Dad told them to get out. However, they kept jabbering and pointing toward home, which was also toward downtown Lamesa. He finally decided they wanted a ride downtown, so he drove there, stopped, and told them to get out. After the Mexicans did a lot of motioning, jabbering, and frantically pointing toward home, Dad got a tire tool from under the seat, and chased them out of his pickup.

It was seventy-five miles from Lamesa, and it took nearly a week for the two Mexicans to find their way home.

Later, sometimes I would jokingly ask, "How about going for a ride in the pickup?"

Their answer was always, "No, Señor, we just want to stay here and work!"

Chapter 29

New Farm, New House, New Job

In 1954 we rented another one hundred sixty acres of land and moved three-quarters of a mile east, to the Rob Hargrove farm where we had a larger house for our growing family.

We made nearly two bales of cotton to the acre that year and thought we would never see another poor day!

Danna started to school that year in Seminole, thirty-five miles from home. Most of the year, she left home before daylight and returned at dark. The other kids on the bus laughed and told us that she slept most of the time each way. She was a great student; and when she got home at night, she taught Debby everything she had learned at school that day.

The Fields family in the mid-fifties.

The girls enjoyed their little brother, carrying or dragging him around until he was two or three years old. After he was housebroke, he became my shadow and stayed with me most of the time. If he wasn't with me, he was following a big bracero named Zeke, who adored David. Beginning at about age three, David and Zeke irrigated many an acre of land together. David got so tanned in the summer, you couldn't tell whether he was our boy or Zeke's.

1955 was more like the first two years we were in the county, dry with lots of wind. We had to replant a lot of cotton that spring, but finally managed to get a crop in. That was the first year we planted sesame, which we grew for three or four years. It was a beautiful crop to grow, and made money, but required much hand labor in the harvesting process. We had to cut it with a broadcast binder, then shock it and feed the bundles into a combine, all by hand. When the Bracero Program was over in 1962, we were

Zeke and David: a perfect picture of mutual admiration

Zeke and David hoe weeds in our yard.

forced to stop growing sesame because there was not enough labor available to harvest it.

That fall, I was elected to the Gaines CountyAgricultural Stabilization Conservation Services (ASCS) County Committee, which administered the cotton allotments and other government programs for the county. Shortly afterward, when everyone had started gathering cotton, the State of Texas ASCS people came into the county and remeasured about two thirds of the cotton which was planted. Many of the allotments were in error, and lots of mistakes had been made in measuring the fields. That caused plenty of hard feelings between the farmers and our three-man county committee.

The State Committee requested our local committee to come to College Station, Texas to meet with them and discuss these problems, but I was the only member who had enough guts to go. I rode to College Station with the County Office Manager, who, along with the Field Supervisor, had overlooked the mistakes and were responsible for the problems. After the way I talked to the Office Manager following the meeting, I wondered if he would make me walk home. The State Committee fired the Fields Supervisor that night, and our local committee fired the Office Manager shortly after we got home. These steps solved the problems and over time ASCS gained more credibility among the local farmers.

CHAPTER 30

A Pox on Me

In the early spring of 1955, four of my neighbors and I were in College Station, Texas for a very important meeting. We were there to meet with the State ASCS Committee. We were growing cotton at the time, and had disagreed with the Gaines County office as to the number of acres we would be allowed to plant that year; so we had appealed our case to the state, and were granted a hearing.

We arrived in College Station after dark; tired from a long trip across the state. I didn't feel just right, but ate supper and went to bed. Some time during the night, I awoke, freezing to death. I was shivering so hard that I was shaking the bed. This continued for a while, then suddenly I was burning up. Then more chills—finally, it dawned on me that I had a high fever. I got out of bed; looked in the mirror and noticed a number of small red blisters on my chest. I knew immediately what was wrong! Our seven year old daughter Danna had brought the chicken pox home from school a couple of weeks before.

I was a busy man, twenty-eight years old and had the damned chicken pox!

The next morning, as the meeting started, I felt awful and my ears were ringing from taking too many aspirin tablets the previous night. The Committeemen were political appointees from across the state, and soon it was apparent that they were not going to waste much time on a bunch of cotton-assed-farmers from Higginbotham, Texas. Our group had asked me to present our case; and as the meeting progressed, I spoke more and more frankly to those bureaucrats. The meeting was both disappointing and unproductive; so when it was over, my parting shot was: "I have the chicken pox, and I hope I have given it to every damned one of you!"

The five hundred mile return trip was a nightmare—more chills and fever—more aspirin. We got home in the wee hours of the morning, and was I glad to be there! I did not get much sleep, however, because about daylight, my Mexican "jefe" (foreman) woke me to help him start one of the irrigation motors. My wife begged me not to go. The temperature was around freezing, and she knew I was really sick; but this was a children's disease and I was tough! I spent a couple of hours in the cold, getting the motor "cranked up."

That was my last trip outside for ten days, except to go to the hospital!

When I got back to the house, Joyce checked my temperature, and it was 103 degrees. She demanded that I go to the doctor, but I said, "No!" She then called two of our friends who had been on the trip to College Station, told them of my condition and asked for help. They came to the house and said, "You can either get in the car with Joyce, or we'll put you in there." As I hobbled to the car, I could feel every sore on the soles of my feet.

Dr. Joe Sharp was a very good friend of ours; and when he saw me, he took one look and fell over laughing. Between fits of laughter, he said, "You look like a damned wetback." I realized then how I was dressed: Levis, boots, western hat, a serape wrapped around my shoulders, and wearing lots of spots. Still laughing, Dr. Sharp looked me over and asked if I had been outside the United States in the last thirty days.

I answered, "No."

He said, "If you had been outside the country, I would say you have small pox. Since you haven't, I'll tell you that you have the worst case of chicken pox I've ever seen. There's not a place on your body that I could put a dime without touching a sore, even the top of your head and the soles of your feet. Your temperature is 104. Go across the street to the hospital, and I'll call them to admit you."

After another argument, I agreed to go and stay until my fever came down.

When I checked into the hospital, I immediately attracted a lot of attention. They told me to take off my clothes and put on a little gown that didn't come to my knees and lacked eight inches coming together in the back. It sure let in a lot of cool air. It was a humiliating experience, and the thought crossed my mind that it would be awful to be found dead, wearing nothing but that thing. It could have been their way of getting me into bed in a hurry. I sure didn't want to be seen in that kind of riggin'.

I must have been quarantined because every time someone came into my room, they put on a coat over their clothes and took it off when they left. They also did a lot of hand washing. I had barely gotten in bed when a young, dumb looking nurse came tripping through the door; not bothering to go through the coat changing routine. She was pushing a suspicious looking cart, which was covered with a sheet, but I could see a lot of red rubber hose under the cover. She started unreeling the hose and cheerfully said, "Turn over on your side, Mr. Machnocker, I need to give you a —— her voice trailed off as she finished the sentence.

I didn't hear what she said, but I thought I knew what she meant. I said, "You're not gonna' give me anything, sister. Get the hell out of here."

She replied, "Dr. Tinley's orders. Please don't give me any trouble."

"My name is Fields, not Machnocker, I'm not Tinley's patient, and you are in the wrong damned room."

"This is room 113, isn't it?," she asked.

"It says 112 on the door behind you."

"Sorry," she said, and rolled her cart out the door, still looking for someone whose garden needed watering.

As she was leaving, another nurse came in with a needle and a tray covered with medicine. After she poked me in the rear with the needle, she said, "Take this."

I swallowed a hand full of pills, drank some liquid, and looked at a double shot glass of thick, pinkish looking stuff. "This too?" I asked.

"Yes," was her answer.

I downed it in about two swallows, but I wasn't sure it would stay where I put it. When I got my breath, I yelled, "Lady, I've drunk lots of bad stuff, but that's the worst thing I've ever had in my mouth. What the hell did you give me?"

"I don't have any idea," she said, "I just do what I'm told."

An hour passed, but the terrible taste in my mouth would not go away. Something seemed familiar about that awful tasting medicine. Finally, a light in my brain began to glow. The empty glass was still sitting on the table. Joyce was nodding off when I said, "Joyce, hand that glass to me." The tone of my voice told her to do as she was told. I took the glass, smelled it, and knew immediately it was the same thing I had rubbed on Danna's sores a few days before. I exclaimed, "That's calamine lotion!"

Joyce said, "Ha, ha, ha. You are hallucinating from your high temperature. It's not calamine lotion."

I replied, "You go to the desk and ask them. I know damned well it is!"

She reluctantly went to check on it, and I could almost hear her when she told the nurse, "My husband thinks he drank calamine lotion; but he didn't, did he?"

Of course, the nurse said, "No."

Joyce returned and said testily, "You did not drink calamine lotion. You are out of your head. Calm down and take a nap. I'm going home to see about the children, and I'll be back later."

I felt worse and worse after she had gone, and finally was so sick at my stomach, I threw up.

After I got back in bed, I was mad enough to bite a ten penny nail in two. I rang the buzzer, and when the same nurse appeared, I said, "Lady, you get your ass down that hall and locate whoever dispensed that pink liquid, and find out if I was supposed to drink it or rub it on. You are going to find out that it was calamine lotion."

Two minutes later, the door flew open and four nurses rushed in, not even bothering to change coats. They were led by the head nurse, who was yelling, "Mr. Fields, you drank calamine lotion. You weren't supposed to drink it. It was to be rubbed on your body to relieve the discomfort of your sores!"

Angrily, I asked, "What the hell have I been telling you for the last three hours?"

She attempted to calm me down by assuring me there was nothing to worry about, because the medicine was harmless. I was not calm, nor was I totally convinced.

Later, when things quieted down, the nurse who had brought the medicine to my room, came in and said, "Mr. Fields, I hope you will believe me when I tell you, that I was ordered to give you that medicine; but if you keep 'raising sand', I am going to lose my job."

I didn't want that to happen, but I could not keep from thinking about those fatal mistakes that happen in hospitals, and how they are covered up.

When Dr. Sharp came by on his rounds, the first thing I said was, "Joe, will that damn stuff they gave me hurt me?"

"What stuff?" he asked.

Before I could answer, the head nurse, who was hiding outside the door to see if I was going to rat on her, rushed into the room. Her voice was about two octaves higher than normal as she hurriedly tried to explain: "Dr. Sharp, the nurse brought some calamine lotion for Mr. Fields to rub on his sores, but he drank it before she could stop him!"

I wanted to call her a liar, but remembered the other nurse might lose her job; so I just grinned, gritted my teeth, and said nothing. It wouldn't have mattered, anyway, because Dr. Sharp was laughing so hard he couldn't have heard me. When he finally regained his composure, he said, "Nah, it won't hurt you."

I was sure, then, that I would be O.K. It might have even been good for me, because by the next day, I was as clean and shiny inside as a tin culvert after a four inch rain. My fever had gone down to one hundred three by the time Joyce got back, and I had had all the hospital treatment I wanted. I said, "Hand me my clothes out of that drawer."

"Why?" she asked.

"I'm going home, that's why."

Joyce threw a fit, and the head nurse was screaming, "I can't check you out without the doctor's permission."

"Tell him I checked myself out," I said, as I went out the door.

Later that night I must have become delirious, because Joyce said I wasn't making any sense when I talked; so she phoned our doctor Joe Sharp at his home.

He said, "Son of a gun, I was afraid of that!," then drove fifteen miles in a blinding sandstorm to bring medicine and see about me.

I was really sick for several days, but as soon as I felt like going to town; I took out a $10,000.00 life insurance policy.

Fifty-six years have gone by, and I've been sick several times, but never considered going back to the hospital.

A burned child is afraid of the fire!

Chapter 31

Ginning Cotton

In the fall of 1955, I had my first experience at working at a cotton gin. The local Paymaster gin had a new manager by the name of J. W. Walters. He was about sixty years old, and I really liked him. Dad and I were ginning our cotton there; so I stopped by late one night, after an ASCS meeting, to see how everything was going. Mr. Walters was at the office by himself; he had been working in the gin all day and weighing trailers at night for two or three days. I felt sorry for him and told him that if he would go home and go to bed, I would weigh the trailers for the rest of the night.

He came in early the next morning with a big smile on his face and said, "Boy! Do I feel good. Reckon you could come back over again tonight?"

I said, "Okay, I'll come back tonight, but you'd better find a night man pretty quick, because I've got all the work I want to do on the farm."

I suspected it at the time, and he told me later that he never looked for anyone else. He strung me out until I got a paycheck, and by then he had me hooked. That was the beginning of a long career in the cotton ginning and related business. I left it thirty-four years later.

1956 was an excellent year for cotton, probably the best one we ever had. Mr. Walters had approached me early in the year and asked me to keep books for him that fall, but I had no bookkeeping experience whatsoever except keeping my own books. He assured me that he would have plenty of people to help me and I would have no problems with the work. That was not exactly true. There was no help; he didn't know anything about the books, so I literally had to dig it out by myself. I burned a lot of midnight oil, and that is the way I learned bookkeeping. It was also the beginning of a friendship between the two of us that lasted throughout his life.

He had two sons working at the gin, Quinton and Hulon. They were both ginners, hard workers, but had no desire to manage the gin. I was thirty years old, a ball of fire, and was sure I could do anything. Mr. Walters liked that and wanted to teach someone what he knew, and he knew a lot. He was a real student of human nature and knew how to get along with people better than anyone I ever knew. He and I never had a cross word in the five years that I worked for him. In addition to managing people, he was a sure enough cotton gin man; so he taught me most of what I know about a gin.

Debby started to school in 1956, but she damned sure didn't sleep on the bus. She was a live wire, if there ever was one. She was as smart as Danna and had learned so much from her that by the time she started to school, she could read and understand an encyclopedia.

When Danna finished the fourth grade, and Debby the second, we transferred them to the Denver City School District. It was only fifteen miles away, so we, having decided to make Denver City our home town, changed our church membership and banking from Lovington, New Mexico to Denver City, Texas. The only problem with transferring the girls was that the Seminole School District would not allow the Denver City buses to enter their district. We had to carry them four miles north to the county line to catch the Denver City school bus. Most of the local children already attended school in Denver City, so we took turns with our neighbors, hauling kids to the county line. Later, several of us bought a little bus and let one of the older kids drive it to the bus line, which was a big help to all of us.

We taught all of our children to drive at an early age. I don't remember for sure about the girls, but David was driving a pickup when he was five, and a tractor when he was seven. That made some of our city friends awfully nervous when their children came to visit us.

I continued to work at the West Gaines Paymaster Gin and to farm, too. I took on one more business, since I didn't have enough to do. Jack McMillan and Jerry Goff were hauling the seed and cotton for the gin, so I bought their three trucks and trailers, their Railroad Commission Permit to haul cotton seed, and I was in the trucking business. I named it State Line Trucks.

Mr. Walters had a heart attack in 1959, so they hired me as Assistant Manager and paid me $350 a month. In 1959 we ginned 7500 bales of cotton, which was pretty good for two old 4-80 saw Murray plants. Mr. Walters retired in 1960, and they made me Manager at $600 per month. I thought that as soon as Mr. Walters was gone, I would gin all the cotton in the country, but that did not happen! When Mr. Walters left the gin, an awful lot of the customers left at the same time. I ginned only 2852 bales of cotton that year. It was a bitter pill to swallow.

I scratched the seat of my pants quite a bit and came up with a plan to gin more cotton in 1961. Thirty-five farmers and I purchased the two gin plants at West Gaines from Paymaster for $185,000.00,

Cotton trailers lined up for ginning on West Gaines Paymaster gin yard.

named it State Line Gins, Inc., and had a very successful year.

I was hired to stay on and manage the two gins for $600 per month. We had a good year in 1961, but after one season, I decided that I had better things to do than work for thirty five crazy farmers. I was still farming and running the trucks, so I had plenty to do. I resigned from the gin in the spring of 1962, and Dan Martin was hired to take my place.

In 1963 Joyce and I bought a neighboring farm from Mr. and Mrs. D.A. Crowder. It rained too much that year, so the crop was short. It was the first time since I had been farming, that I had ever failed to repay my bank loan. It didn't worry me very much, because I was sure that I would pay come out the next year.

I bought quite a bit of equipment during 1964 and 1965. I purchased two new truck tractors, several used trucks and trailers, and some more Railroad Commission authority so I would be able to haul additional commodities and oil field equipment. Again, I was unable to pay my loan at the bank.

By the middle sixties, most of our neighbors had bought sprinkler systems which certainly made a difference in their farming operations. It saved a lot of labor, fuel, and water. We were still running water down the rows, which took a lot of hand labor and hard work. Since we did not own the land, we didn't feel able to purchase the sprinkler systems ourselves. We had the best landlords in the world, but they could not see the problem of our needing a sprinkler system. I was making a lot of money for them but not for myself. I know they thought I was making money too, but I was spending too much of my own money making a crop.

When I went to the bank in March of 1966, I was told that they would no longer finance my operation. Later I realized that I had been caught in a power struggle at the bank, but that didn't put any money in my account.

We were forced to quit farming. We auctioned off all our farm equipment, but I was able to save the trucking business. My folks moved back to Snyder, and we moved to a place south of Denver City.

Joyce got a job at the bank to help out. We had an awfully hard time for several years. There were many times when I wondered how I was going to put food on the table for the family, but I always managed to do so. I didn't see much of the family for a few years because I was on the road day and night. I could have quit trucking and got a job, but I knew I'd never be able to pay our notes at the bank on a salary, since I owed them so much money. Bankruptcy would have been the simple solution, but I didn't even consider it, because I had borrowed the money and was determined to pay it back. I was not able to pay much on my note in 1967, so they told me that if 1968 was not better, they would foreclose on my trucks. A little Mexican named Merced and I hauled 40,000 bales of hay during the summer of 1968, and my rear got down to about the width of a notebook. The bales weighed 80 to 90 pounds each, and they damned near ruined my disposition. Late that summer, I told one of my bankers how I had done financially and how the rest of the year looked. I asked him if a certain amount of money would be satisfactory for the year.

He said, "What difference does it make?"

I answered, "It makes a hell lot of difference to me!"

He asked, "If It's not enough money, and we decide to foreclose, what do you think you're going to do?"

I replied, "I'm going to see if another bank will loan me the money to pay you off."

Sneering, he said, "Who do you think would loan you any money?"

I was hotter than a pistol when I said, "I don't know, but I've been told "no" by a damned sight better banker than you are, so I'm going to do a lot of driving and talking to bankers. If you think for one minute that I am going to sit on my ass and howl while you foreclose on me, you're the silliest son of a bitch in Yoakum County!"

The bank charged off my note, never again asked me to pay them, and tried to help me any way they possibly could.

Nine years later, I payed them every nickel I had borrowed, plus interest.

Chapter 32

Hangin' On and Hangin' in There

Our kids were all good students and very involved in extracurricular activities at school. Danna played in the band and was a drum majorette, finishing third in her class at graduation. Debby sang in the choir and was a cheerleader. David played baseball and football, until he injured his elbow and was forced to quit sports. For these reasons, we were on the road, back and forth to town, most of the time.

1966 through 1970 were tough years for us. In addition to all the other hardships, Dad died in '67, and our children were growing up and leaving home. Danna married Robert Dewlen and they left for college at the University of Texas in Austin in the fall of 1966. Debby

Danna, Dan and Debby pose, ready for a football game.

started to college at Texas Tech in 1968, and David rode off into the sunset in 1970.

Every time one of them went away it left a big hole in the hearts of the rest of our family, since we were so close. Some parents are glad when their children leave home, but we most certainly were not in that category. Robert graduated from college in 1969 with an engineering degree, and the best present we could give him at the time was a greeting card. However, I wrote a poem for him on a piece of cardboard, Joyce added a bit of art work and we framed it with ornamental aluminum. The poem read as follows:

Congratulations,
My son-in-law!
I'll try not to mind
If you call me Pa.

The hard times gone,
The days are sunny.
I'm glad to know
You are in the money.

I trust you'll support me,
When my trucks are busted
In the style I'd like
To become adjusted.

How about a private
Swimming pool?
And I've always wanted
To dress real cool.

The grooviest clothes
That money can buy
(You know, the kind
That catch the eye).

I'd like the best:
The steaks T-bone,
A jug to call
My very own.

In the upper crust
There is a law.
You need to be proud
Of your father-in-law.

If engineering should
Make you rich,
I'll pretend you're not
A Son of A Bitch.

That was almost forty years ago. He still has the card, shows it to his friends with pride, and he's a real son to me.

The gin, which by then was called State Line Cooperative, had fallen on hard financial times after I left as manager. The directors thought I could "pull it out of the hole"; but in 1969, when they asked me if I'd take the job as manager again, I said, "Hell no! I wouldn't run that 'wore out son of a bitch' for all the rice in China!"

Then they asked, "How much money would it take to hire you to manage the gin? You can continue operating your trucking business."

I thought of a figure which I didn't think they could pay or that their banker would allow if they wanted to.

I said, "$800 per month, a house, a pickup and expenses." They took me up on the deal, and I stayed there twenty years.

Chapter 33

The Big Black Steer

"Watch out, Pop," I yelled, "That black son-of-a-bitch will hit you!"

Dad scrambled up the corral fence as the big black steer came tearing down the stockyard alley in a dead run. I chuckled as I thought to myself, "Dad looks more like 32 than 72 years old." He was helping us cut out some big Mexican Brahman steers in the stockyards of El Paso, Texas. We were there in the spring of 1958, where five years later, President John F. Kennedy met the President of Mexico and signed an agreement giving several hundred acres of land to Mexico. The land, given to settle an old border dispute, was part of the city of El Paso, including the stockyard area, and is now known as El Chamizal.

Dad and I were partners in the farming and ranching business. We were in the market for some steers, and so was one of our neighbors, Bill Green. We learned that the Ziegler Cattle Company in El Paso had a bunch for sale, so Bill and I had driven out there the day before to check them out.

We found Ziegler's office in the old Paso Del Norte Hotel, where we were introduced to Mr. Hagler, their manager. He told us they had two hundred and eighty steers they had purchased in the Mexican State of Coahuila. They brought them across the Rio Grande at Eagle Pass, Texas, and from there they were shipped by rail to El Paso. He took us to the stockyards to take a look at them, and we really liked their looks. They were Brahman, mostly two-year-olds, with a few threes, and wilder than an acre of snakes. The colors ran from white to brown, a half dozen spotted, and a big black one with a bad disposition. He was as conspicuous as a rat turd in a bran sack, so he was the particular steer I remember.

Ziegler had owned the steers for quite a while, so with the cost of the cattle, feed and freight, they had a lot of money in them. Because of this, Mr. Hagler made it clear that a good price could be negotiated. After some dickering, we made him an offer, subject to Dad's approval, and he took us up on the price.

When I called Dad to give him my report on the cattle, he decided to catch the bus to El Paso to help finalize the trade. That night, as Bill and I sat around the Greyhound Bus Station waiting for Dad, a couple of loud mouthed Yankees sitting behind us began to shoot off their mouths about cowboys. It didn't take much of that to get the hair on the back of my neck to standing straight out, so when one of them raised his voice and said, "When I get back home, I'm going to tell everyone I saw two real cowboys from Texas," I retorted, "When I get home, I'm going to tell everyone I saw two ignorant 'sons-a-

The big black steer.
(Courtesy of Southwest Collection, Texas Tech University)

bitches' from New Jersey." I got ready to "clean their plow," in case a fight broke out, but that stopped the mouthing.

By sun-up the next morning, we were in the cattle pens, where Dad gave his O.K. on the steers. Bill wanted a fourth of them and we took the rest. We finalized the trade, arranged for trucks, and were separating the cattle by 10:00 A.M.

Dad had won a coin toss with Bill to decide who got the first cut; we would take the first three, then Bill got one, and so on until we were finished. I walked into the corral to make the first cut, picked out two of the biggest steers and headed them toward the gate Bill was tending. When the big black steer saw the gate was open, he almost ran over the other two in his rush to get ahead, and I realized later that the "black bastard," as he was unaffectionately named, always had to be the first one through a gate. He snorted once and shook his horns at Dad as he ran by. It was a good thing that Pop had stepped up on the side of the fence.

We paid for the cattle, fixed up the papers which allowed the cattle to be hauled through the corner of New Mexico, loaded them into the trucks, and headed for home. As we passed the trucks leaving El Paso, we noted that they made quite a convoy of bull-hauling rigs.

Bill, Dad and I made it home about sundown and figured the trucks would be a couple of hours behind us, but cattle trucks are like babies; they are always late and come in the middle of the night. Four hours later, they arrived—having been detained at the Carlsbad, New Mexico Port Of Entry. The unloading went smoothly. As each truck was unloaded, we counted the steers and held them in the corral for a bit, until they settled down.

We then turned them into a trap (a small pasture), where they were supposed to stay until morning, but when the last truck backed in to unload, I called to Dad, "Open the gate, I'll count 'em as they come down the chute!"

"Aren't you going to hold this load in the corral for a minute?" he asked.

"No, I'm tired and ready to go to the house; they'll be O.K. Open the gate!"

"All right, but it's not a good idea."

Dad was right, as usual. Those steers came flying down the chute, through the corral, and into the trap where they disappeared into the darkness!

It had been a long day, I was tired, and Dad was exhausted as each of us headed for home. Little did we realize that the day was just beginning. Neither of us had time to clean up before my phone began to ring off the wall. Most of our neighbors knew that Dad and I had been off on a cattle buying trip, so when some of them heard their dogs barking and the sound of cattle running, they knew who to call.

I phoned Pop and said, "Get your boots back on, I think those son-of-bitching steers have stampeded!"

By the time Dad and I had loaded up in our pickups and were ready to roll, Bill had come over to offer his help. First, we checked the trap and saw by the headlights of the pickup that the steers were gone! We soon realized they were scattered all over the country. We located several small bunches, but decided to leave them until daylight and try to find the big end of the herd. We finally found one big bunch going down Texas Highway 1757, headed back toward El Paso. That was a dangerous situation; midnight had passed, and most of the eastbound traffic on the highway was coming from Dan's Bar, four or five miles to the west. Dan's was an area "watering hole" in the edge of New Mexico where West Texans went to drink and buy beer and liquor, since it was not sold in that part of Texas. Anyone venturing out on Texas State Highway 1757 or New Mexico Highway 133 after 10:00 o'clock at night was taking his life in his own hands, since ninety percent of the drivers going east were half crocked and driving fast.

While we tried to decide on a plan, we saw a couple of near misses between cars and cattle; so we quickly ran the steers through a gate into a 30 section pasture on the Higginbotham Ranch. It was a good feeling to get at least part of the cattle off the highway, but we knew the big end of the herd was still missing. One of the homeward bound drunks stopped and told us, "You guys sure missed a hell of a lot of excitement at Dan's Bar a while ago!"

Someone had called the New Mexico State Police to report a large number of cattle on the highway; so a State Trooper had come out, seen the cattle, turned on his siren, and the race was on. When the beer drinkers heard the siren, several of them rushed outside the bar to see what was taking place, and were nearly run over by the frightened cattle.

The drunk continued, "You should have seen it! I never saw so damned many wild cattle in my life! I nearly got run over by a big black son-of-a-bitch that was leading the herd! They crossed Highway 122 in a dead run and didn't kill a soul!"

When we finally caught up with that bunch, they were ten miles from home and had covered the ground in record time. They were still moving and headed toward Mexico. We herded them into a wheat field, where Bill and I held them until morning. We had sent Dad home to rest, but by first light he was back with saddle horses, sandwiches and coffee. Boy, did that food taste good! We ate, saddled up and started pushing the cattle toward home. We didn't have any idea how many cattle were still missing or where they might be, so Dad took off for Seminole, Texas, the county seat of Gaines County to register the HP brand the steers were carrying. That would settle any question of ownership until we could put our XU brand on them.

We had driven the cattle four or five miles when Dad returned, accompanied by the sheriff of Gaines County, who had no jurisdiction in New Mexico but came as a friend in case we had a problem with bringing the cattle across the state line. We almost had another stampede as we passed Dan's Bar where three or four of the morning drunks were outside, whistling and yelling like TV cowboys.

Somewhere along the way back home, we were joined by ten or twelve friends and neighbors coming to help out. They had rounded up every old plug horse in the community and were having a ball. They were good farm people; but most of them had little knowledge of cows, and some of them weren't sure which end a cow ate with. They had come to help us but decided they might as well have a good time, so it turned into a festive occasion. It was "Riders of the Purple Sage," "Home On The Range," and "Gunsmoke," all rolled into one. We made quite a procession led by the sheriff, then the black bastard leading the other steers, several cowboys (or "would-be cowboys"), then last came Dad and a couple of other men pulling horse trailers.

The rest of the trip was made without event, and I breathed a big sigh of relief as old "Blackie" led the steers back into the trap which they had broken out of the night before. Our Mexican hired hands had rebuilt the fence and seen to it that there was plenty of feed and water for the cattle. We figured that the last load of steers, which I had hurriedly released the night before, had spooked the rest of the nervous herd as they ran into the trap, sending them crashing through the fence.

The rest of the day, we gathered up several small bunches of cattle and, by nightfall, hoped that the only ones still missing were in the Higginbotham pasture. Thank Goodness for a hot supper and a good bed! We had been on the go for 36 hours and sure needed some rest.

The cowboys gathered early the next morning and we got ready to ride the five by six mile pasture on the Higginbotham Ranch, where we had left some of the steers the night before. As I sat on my horse, waiting for the rest of the "Bonanza Bunch" to mount up, I watched my friend Ritter Holder out of the corner of my eye. He had borrowed an old beat up saddle that was held together with binder twine and baling wire, and was saddling up a small borrowed filly that I called a kid pony. Like most horses ridden by amateur riders or children, she was spoiled. Ritter was a big, two hundred and sixty pound man, and the little filly had carried him a long way the day before; so maybe she didn't want to haul him around for another one. At any rate, each time Ritter attempted to put his foot in the stirrup to mount, the pony would halfheartedly kick at him with her left hind foot. It was not a typical horse kick which might cause serious injury; it was to send a message to children that they couldn't ride that day. Ritter knew nothing about horses; so each time the filly kicked, he would step back, and then try again. I could hardly keep from laughing out loud as I watched but said nothing. Finally, the filly decided she'd had enough fun and allowed Ritter to mount. During this time, the rest of the "Bonanza" crew had gone on ahead of us, then some of Ritter's riggin' broke, which caused him to lose his stirrup and everything tied to it. We found some wire, repaired the stirrup leather, and Ritter reached for the stirrup with his foot—another kick—another try—same thing! Ritter was a jovial fellow, always happy, and never "out of sorts;" but at this particular moment, the back of his neck was turning red, so I knew he was "heating up." I sat on my horse, smiling, but again I said nothing. Suddenly, Ritter's head jerked around. He looked at me and said, "What the hell would you do if you were me?"

Calmly, I replied, "I'd kick the belly off that little son-of-a-bitch!"

That was what Ritter wanted to hear. He grabbed the cheek of the horse's bridle, and Kaboom!—his right foot disappeared in the pony's belly, and all four of her feet came off the ground at the same time. The horse kicking continued for a couple of minutes, and I couldn't decide whether it sounded like distant cannon fire or someone beating a bass drum. When the noise stopped, the filly looked in the other direction; as if to say, "Please, get on!" Smart horse!

Our group spread out and covered roughly one-fourth of the big pasture by noon that day, but the only cattle we saw belonged to the Higginbotham Ranch. When lunch time came we returned to my house where my wife, Joyce, and my mother had cooked a big meal for the entire crew.

We were a little slower when we went back to work. My cowboys were unaccustomed to riding horseback and were beginning to get stiff and sore. Somehow the glitter was wearing off the roundup, along with a little hide from their rear ends. Two or three of them pulled out for home. We rode another quarter of the pasture that afternoon, but still had no luck in finding the Brahmans.

The next morning as we prepared to set out once more, suddenly there was a deafening Z000000M above us! It was another friend—Willard Freeman in his airplane. He had come in behind us about fifteen feet off the ground, so no one heard the plane until it was over us. Some of the horses spooked, and one farmer was unloaded from his horse; so he was immediately dubbed "round ass," a name which stuck with him for a long time. I could almost hear Willard laughing as he banked the plane and came in for a landing on the highway.

Tears ran down his face as he said, "That's the best rodeo I've seen since I went to the Ft. Worth Fat Stock Show!" He went on to tell us that he had heard what we were doing and said, "Dan, tell me what to look for, and I'll find the cattle in ten minutes."

(left to right) Preston Underhill, Robbie Fleming, (unknown), (unknown), Bill Green, Dee Freeman, Travis Pharr, Willard Freeman (pilot) and Jerry Goff. Front row, Sidney Underhill All standing in front of Willard's airplane, used to find the last of the strays.

Neighbors enjoying Joyce and Mom's cooking after a hard day of branding cattle.

I described them and explained that they would be easy to recognize since the Higginbotham cattle were all Black Angus, while ours were a lighter color.

Willard took off, headed south, and in a few minutes returned waggling his wings, so we knew he had spotted the steers. He led us to the southwest corner of the pasture, where we found them. It may have been coincidental that this bunch too, had drifted back in the direction of Mexico. We headed them north and by sundown had them back home. We counted the steers, and all 210 of them were accounted for. We hadn't lost a one!

Branding the cattle went smoothly the next day. We had plenty of help and spectators, too. Joyce and Mom had cooked half of the night before and really put on a big "feed" at noon. We ate lunch under the trees, rested for a while and "hurrawed" some of the cowboys for letting "little bitty" steers run them up the fence. Then, still full as a tick, we slowly went back to work.

I had noticed that morning when we loaded the chute with cattle to start the branding, that there was one gate the black steer didn't

Dan ear marking cattle.

go through first. Evidently, he had "been there and done that," and could remember it by the HP that had been burned into the hide on his hip. He spent the day in the back side of the pen, minding his own business, and occasionally making a pass at some cotton-assed farmer who walked in front of him. At last we were down to the final five or six head, and "Old Blackie's" time was up; so with much yelling, cussing, and arm-waving, we had that black son-of-a-gun in the chute. He didn't like the smell of blood and burning hair; so when he hit the steel squeeze chute, he really tested the material in it. I put the red-hot iron on Blackie's left side; purposely held it a few extra seconds to get even with him, then when the smoke cleared, I stepped back and admired our XU brand.

Dad was marking ears, and he sometimes got carried away with his job. When I saw him cut off nearly a fourth of each of the black steer's ear, I said, "Godamighty, Pop! Don't take so much ear. You're ruining their looks."

"I can see the mark when I ride up on one of 'em," he retorted.

"Yeah," I said, "You can see the ear mark before you can see the steer!"

Of course, he continued to do as he wanted.

We finished up branding, opened the gate and turned the steers out into the pasture. Dad and I thanked all our help; and as they cleared out, we breathed a sigh of relief. We were anxious to go home; but we took time for one more look at the cattle, and liked what we saw. They were a good bunch of steers; we had bought them right and wondered if we'd ever see another poor day! We had put in a rough four days. We were worn out, and so were the steers. I'll bet when they bedded down that night, they had a lot to talk about!

I spent a lot of time on a horse that year; but as the end of summer came, and our grass began to play out, I rode more and more, keeping the Brahmans at home. They had little respect for fences; so when they spotted some grass, they didn't care whether it was in our pasture or not.

Dad stopped by one day to tell me, "That damned old black steer is out of the pasture again."

I saddled up, located him and started him toward the corral, which was only a quarter of a mile away. The only problem was that I wanted him to go north while he intended to go south. Back and forth we went for a while. I had "choused" him pretty hard; he was hot and mad, and so was I. Finally, I said to myself, "I'll show you, you black bastard!" I built a loop, roped him and was attempting to drive him, on the end of the rope, toward the corral, when I saw Vicente, one of our braceros (a legalized Mexican National) coming on foot to help me.

"Cuidado, Vicente," I said, "Esta poco caliente!"

That was an understatement. Old Blackie was more than a "little hot!" He took one look at Vicente, lowered his head, and went after his Mexican ass! There was slack in my rope; my horse set himself for the wreck, and when the big steer hit the end of the rope, it snapped. In his rush to avoid the hard-charging steer, Vicente fell down, and Old Blackie was on him like a duck on a June bug! Vicente had rolled himself into a little ball, trying to be invisible, but it didn't work. The old steer began to enthusiastically shine his head, horns and hooves on Vicente's rear end! It probably took no more than a minute for me to tie another knot in my rope; drop a loop over the steer's horns and pull him away, but for Vicente it was a long time. He was skinned up a little, but nothing serious was wrong with him. His feelings were hurt more than anything else; because when I tried to be sympathetic, all I could do was laugh. With very little help from that hombre, I finally got the steer back where he belonged. I named Vicente the "torrero" (bull fighter), but after his roughing up, he was never worth much around cattle.

The time came when we had to move some of the steers. Feed was short, so I was relieved when an old friend of mine called to offer some help. Marshall Neville ranched fifteen miles south of McCamey, Texas, and was one of the best people I've known. He was getting along in years, and had spent his life where everything that grows has stickers. He was as crusty as a sourdough biscuit baked in a dutch oven.

He said, "Fields, I can't help you much, but I've got room for one hundred or so of your Brahmans for thirty, maybe forty-five days."

Early the next morning we were loading cattle to go to Marshall's ranch. We opened the gate to separate the steers going south, and which one do you think went through the gate first? You guessed it—the black one! Then when the gate to the chute was opened, he charged through it, up the chute and into the cattle truck; but as soon as he saw that it was a trap, out he came. We loaded the steers several times, because each time, before we could close the gate in the back of the truck, Old Blackie was out again. Finally, I told the truck driver to hand me a hotshot, which is an electrical prod and not usually recommended for Brahman cattle. They are inclined to wreck things when shocked, but drastic situations call for drastic measures! Once more we loaded all the steers except the black one. I headed him toward the chute and yelled, "Look out boys, I'm fixin' to load this son-of-a-bitch!" I slipped up behind him and placed the hotshot against the tenderest part of his anatomy, and pulled the trigger. A flying hoof went by my head as he kicked like a blue-nosed mule, but I continued to hold the "juice" to him as far up the chute as I could run. He plowed into the other cattle far enough for me to slam the gate. He was loaded!!

I caught up with the cattle trucks as they were pulling into Odessa, Texas, and my heart skipped a beat or two when I saw the black steer jump up and put his head and front feet on the top rail of the cattle trailer. I was positive he was going to jump; it was just a matter of where and when. I wondered what I would do if he got loose in downtown Odessa. I had a 45 caliber pistol with me——should I shoot him? All my worrying was in vain because when the trucks left town he dropped back down in the trailer with the rest of the cattle. He was a country steer and apparently was just enjoying the view of the city.

When we unloaded at Marshall's ranch, the trucks backed into a ditch, and we jumped the cattle out into the pasture, rather than drive them three or four miles from the pens at his house. For the last time, Old Blackie was first out and hit the ground running.

The steers which were left at home, we shipped to San Angelo, Texas, and ran them through the auction. We were somewhat disappointed with the price they brought, but that's the way the cow business works.

The steers at McCamey had done well; but as the time came to move them, I dreaded driving them the three or four miles through heavy brush to the pens at Marshall's ranch house.

Earlier, Marshall had told me, "Dan, I have two Mexican cowboys who can help us, so the four of us can handle them, but it won't be a cinch with those "spooky cattle." He then expressed an interest in buying the steers range delivery (where they were located).

I went to see him early one morning and told him I would like to sell him the cattle, if he was still interested. If not, we would gather them that day and ship them to the San Angelo auction the next. This started a good-natured cow trade that went on and on. Three hours later, we had gotten to a point where we were apart by only

$5.00 a head. Finally, in exasperation, I said, "Marshall, I've come down on the price all I'm going to; if you want the steers, it'll be at my price. I'm through arguing!"

He snapped back, "Let's catch them goddamned horses, and we'll gather your steers! You can take them to San Angelo!"

I had to laugh; I knew I was out-traded. I said, "Write me a check, at your price and I'll go home. That'll put me out of the Brahman steer business."

The story on these steers was the same as those sold in San Angelo. The market had weakened, and the money didn't quite reach. Dad and I had worked and worried a lot of the year for nothing, but that's "La Vida."

I saw Marshall at a funeral several years later and we had time for a brief visit. He joshingly inquired, "Fields, have you got any more Brahman cattle for sale?"

I retorted, "I wasn't sure you had gathered the last ones I sold you."

"Well," he said, "I got all of them but one. We were bringing them to the house when a big black son-of-a-bitch broke out of the herd; and as one of the cowboys tried to turn him, he jumped my south fence into a neighbor's ranch. It was a few days before we started looking for him; and by that time, he was gone. We couldn't imagine what might have happened to him."

Dan's registered brand: an XU on the cow's left side.

Marshall went on to say, "Two or three years later, I ran into a friend of mine in Fort Stockton, who has a ranch about thirty-five miles south of me. He told me he heard that I had lost a big black steer. I said, 'I did, but he's been gone a long time. He's carrying my brand, and also an XU and an HP, which are Dan Fields' brands."

His friend said, "He's down on my outfit, come and get him when you have time, but bring plenty of help, 'cause he's 'one snakey muther!' I'll bet the son-of-a-bitch weighs two thousand pounds, and he's wilder'n a shit-house mouse! Heh, heh, a couple of drug-store-cowboys from Ozona, roped him a while back, and some of their riggin' is still scattered around over my south pasture!"

"He's your steer," Marshall replied. "You can keep him, shoot him, or whatever else you want to do, but I don't want a damned thing to do with him. I'm sure as hell not comin' after him!"

I can picture in my mind, that several years later, a lonely Mexican was perched on a rocky hill in Northern Mexico. He was watching a crossing on the Rio Bravo, or Rio Grande, as the gringos call it, waiting for darkness to cover his illegal entry into the United States. He idly puffed on a cigarette as he watched carefully for the hated "chota" (U. S. Border Patrol). Suddenly, he stiffened as he saw something move in the heavy brush along the opposite side of the river, but it was only a tired, sore footed, old black steer that emerged from the brush. The steer walked slowly down the bank, then waded a short distance into the river, lowered his head, and drank deeply. Raising his big head, he looked up and down the river, and slowly crossed to the Mexican side. It appeared that his steps quickened slightly as he climbed the bank of the Rio Bravo and disappeared up the trail which led in the direction of his home in the Mexican State of Coahuila.

What had driven him? Had some innate sense always directed him toward home? He had almost come full circle. He had been shipped by rail 500 miles west to El Paso, trucked 250 miles northeast to Higginbotham, hauled another 200 miles south to McCamey, and then walked south another 80 miles. By the time he reached the Rio Bravo, he had traveled more than 1000 miles in the United States, a long way for a Mexican steer without a passport or a travel agent.

Chapter 34

High Jumping Bull

I stopped one afternoon to see my friend Marshall Neville, south of McCamey, Texas, to visit for a while. He told me he had sold a big Brahman bull to a rancher from Sanderson, Texas, and was waiting for him to come and pick him up. While we were visiting, the fellow drove up in what we called a six wheel truck, with an open top, thirty four foot trailer, certainly not what we would have picked out to haul a big bull; but as Marshall said, "It's his bull."

He backed his trailer up to the chute, paid Marshall for the bull, and we got ready to load him. When we were ready to run him up the chute, Marshall said, "Feller, ain't you gonna' tie that bull?"

"Nah" said the rancher, "He'll be all right."

Marshall said, "O.K., he's your bull."

We ran the old bull up the chute; he never slowed down as he ran through the trailer, jumped out over the corner of the nose of the trailer and hit the ground with a smack. Amazingly, he was not injured. He then loped off into the edge of the pasture and started to graze. The old bull was gentle, and two of Marshall's Mexican cowboys went out and brought him back into the corral.

Again, we got ready to drive the bull up the chute; and Marshall said, "Feller, you ought to tie that bull."

The rancher replied, "Ah, that was just a fluke. He'll be OK. Run him in there."

Marshall said, "OK, he's still your bull."

The same thing happened, the bull ran through the trailer and again jumped out over the front corner, again hitting the ground, hard.

That happened one more time, except that time the bull went out over the middle of the front of the trailer. He hit the cab of the tractor, mashed in the top, kicked out the windshield, and caved in the hood. He again loped out into the pasture and began to graze.

When we drove the bull up the chute the last time, the rancher turned to Marshall and asked, "Marshall how do you think we oughta' tie that bull?"

Chapter 35

Horsin' Around on Christmas Eve

A wonderful thing happened on Christmas Eve of 1964.

The night was bitterly cold in Higginbotham, Gaines County, Texas. My wife was wrapping last minute packages while our three children, Danna, Debby and David were busily shaking their many gifts, trying to decide what was inside each of them. I was lounging in my easy chair, taking mental inventory of how many bicycles and toys would have to be assembled after the children were asleep.

Suddenly there was a sharp knock at the door. I glanced at the clock. It was 9:30 P.M. and as I made my way to the door, I wondered who would be calling so late on this special night. Could it be Santa Claus? Not likely! I opened the door, and there stood Bill, one of my hired hands, grinning rather sheepishly.

I said, "What's up, Bill? Come in out of the cold."

He replied, "Well, I came after that Shetland filly colt that you said you'd sell me on credit. That's going to be all my kids get for Christmas."

My mind flashed back a month or more. We had been working together; and he had casually asked, "Dan, what would you take for that mouse colored colt of yours?"

"Fifty dollars," I answered.

He explained, "I might not be able to pay you for awhile."

I said, "I guess that would be O.K."

That conversation certainly did not constitute a "horse trade," so I had completely forgotten it.

I really wanted to tell Bill to go home, and come back another time, but I remembered his seven, small, stair-stepped children, and after all, it was Christmas. He was in a bind, so all I said was, "You picked a helluva time to take delivery, Bill!"

I got out my warmest coat, put on my gloves, and pulled my hat down tight. Together, Bill and I headed out into the cold, black night. A few flakes of snow were falling, and the wind was blowing 25 miles an hour. As we passed the thermometer, I shined a small flashlight on it. It registered 20 degrees. What a bitch of a night to be outside!

The pickup complained a little bit, but finally started. We hooked my old open-topped horse trailer to the pickup and headed for the pasture where we kept the horses.

As we drove along, I wondered if we were going to be able to pen the horses in the dark. Fortunately, that afternoon I had closed the gate on a ten acre trap, holding the horses in there; so that gave us a pretty good chance of penning them.

We arrived at the pasture and shined the lights of the pickup on the gate of the corral, then lit out on foot to try to drive the horses into the pens. It was so dark that the lights of the pickup didn't help much. We could hear the running horses, but only saw them when they passed the gate a couple of times and then ran back into the darkness.

While we were chasing the horses around the pasture, I thought about an old neighbor, whom I had stopped to see one day. He had chased an old saddle horse around a small pasture for about two hours and was worn out, hot, and mad. He was a very religious man, but at this point some of his spirituality had begun to slip away. He said, "It's a strange thing to me that the Lord made heaven and earth and gave man dominion over them and everything therein, and not a damn thing he could outrun!"

My thoughts returned to the job at hand as the horses came around for the third time and an old mare finally led them into the pens. Then we closed the gate and began to get down to business.

The first thing we had to do was to cut the pony out from the rest of the horses and get her into another pen. We moved the pickup around so we had a little better light.

If this had been a wild, full sized colt, we would have fore-footed it, which meant roping its front feet, jerking them out from under it two or three times. This would knock the wind out of it and get its attention. However, this was a Shetland pony, so we knew we could handle her with a rope around her neck. The two-year-old colt had only been roped once in her life . . . when I had caught her, thrown her down and trimmed her feet. That's the only time she had been handled.

We dropped a loop around her neck and the battle was on. She literally went crazy, out there in the dark, squealing, biting and kicking. We wrestled around with her, finally got a hackamore on her head and drug her into the trailer. We tied her securely, and headed out for Bill's house. It was about 11:00 o'clock by this time, and the weather wasn't warming up any.

We drove up to Bill's house, and the show started! The door burst open and out came all those seven children, screaming with delight. Some with coats on, some without, but none of them noticed the cold. They hit the side of the trailer and were climbing all over it. Of course, the frightened pony was having a wall-eyed fit. Bill was yelling for them to get away from the trailer, but to no avail. He would scrape kids off one side of the trailer, and while he went to the other side, the original bunch were back on it again. They were even trying to get into the trailer to get on the horse. I was positive a kid or two were going to get killed.

I still don't know how we ever got that pony unloaded, with all the confusion, but we did, and tied her to a tree in the yard. I figured that by morning there would be a lot of mangled kids lying around.

When I finally arrived back home, it was midnight, and the family was still up, romping and stomping. I called them together and with tears in my eyes shared my story with them. I said, "I've seen a real Christmas tonight. We are all so fortunate! We have so many blessings and so many gifts. We are spoiled, and take Christmas for granted. I witnessed the real meaning of Christmas tonight, and I'll never forget it."

I went back to Bill's house the day after Christmas, expecting to see a few bodies lying around. Wrong! The colt was completely broken! The kids had teamed up, some of them leading the colt and two riding it. The pony was broke to lead and ride. It was completely gentle. All this had been done in thirty-six hours. I knew they had tormented it day and night since it arrived and had worn it completely down.

Three or four months later, Bill, his family and the colt drifted on. He never found the money to pay me, but the gift I received was many times greater than the price of a horse.

PART IV

Trucking, Ginning and Surviving

CHAPTER 36

The Last of the Big Buffalo Traders

Until Lyndon B. Johnson became the 36th President of the United States in 1963, not many people had paid attention to the small herd of buffalo which he kept on his Johnson City Ranch. However, as more folks stopped to see the home of the President, they were moved by the sight of the magnificent animals grazing along the Pedernales River. Interest in buffalo increased and soon the ownership of them became a status symbol in the Hill Country of Texas, creating a hot market for these strange looking creatures. This confirmed my theory that a lot of people have more money than sense.

Two of the last buffalo traded.

As far as I know, there are only three reasons for the buffalo's existence:

1. To be looked at and photographed
2. To tear down fences
3. To feed and clothe Indians

Except for these reasons, a buffalo is as useless as teats on a boar hog.

When it became apparent to me that people were serious about buying buffalo and had money, I rigged up a "Bison Buggy," which was a strong livestock trailer covered by a fence panel chained to the top. This lid prevented the buffalo from jumping out.

Next, I started scouting West Texas and Eastern New Mexico for this four footed commodity. I found a few small herds; but over the next couple of years, my primary sources of supply were the Linam Ranch west of Hobbs, New Mexico, the Snyder Ranch west of Arkansas Junction, New Mexico and the Ty Field Ranch at Bronco, Texas.

The first load I purchased came from the Linam and Snyder Ranches and was sold to a businessman-rancher near Johnson City, Texas. I was never very good at math, so when I figured what my margin of profit should be, I decided on 2 per cent. I bought the buffalo for $150.00 each and sold them for $300.00 apiece. I had also made arrangements with the buyer to purchase some Spanish goats for me—several nannies and a billy so I could raise some goats to barbecue. (Um—that cabrito is good stuff!)

Our son, David, was 10 years old at the time and helped me rig up the trailer. The idea of hauling buffalo was "big doings" for him; and he casually mentioned that if I could make the trip on a weekend, he felt sure that he could arrange his business so that he could go with me. I agreed, and we invited his friend Bart Kelley to go with us. Bart was delighted.

We loaded the first buffalo at the Snyder outfit without incident, then went on to the Linam Ranch, arriving about 10:00 o'clock on

David Fields and Bart Kelley along side the "Bison Buggy."

Saturday morning. Things began to happen, problems developed and we didn't get away until up in the afternoon. The cowboys had trouble penning the herd, and we had some problems loading the ones I had bought. We could not rope and tie them in the trailer for fear of killing them by collapsing their windpipes, so we had to drive all of them into the buggy at the same time. This would not have been a problem with cattle, but it seemed that about half of the buffalo's heads were on the wrong end. When half of them were going into the trailer, the other half were coming out. A chicken has more sense than a buffalo, but I guess it is natural for them to violently resist being enclosed.

When we finally got loaded, Mrs. Linam asked me if I would go on down to the 9 Bar Ranch, just northwest of Houston and bring back a registered Santa Gertrudis bull for her after delivering the buffalo. The pay was good, so I agreed, but it changed my plans for the trip, especially with a late start.

I began to wish the boys had not come along, because this extended the trip to eleven-hundred miles and they had to be in school on Monday. We held a conference and they assured me that we could make it back on time. I think they would have died if I had taken them back home, and it would have added another hundred miles to my trip.

We "set sail" and got to the Johnson City Ranch about 10:00 o'clock Saturday night, unloaded the buffalo, loaded the goats and hit the road again. We finally stopped at Hempstead to sleep for a couple of hours.

The sun was coming up when we drove through the gate at the 9 Bar Ranch. I looked the bull over that we were to pick up and saw that he weighed about 2000 pounds and was too tall to fit under the lid of the "Bison Buggy." The boys and I dismantled the top and chained it to the side of the trailer.

Time was passing, but we took a few minutes for the manager of the ranch to show us around the place. What a beautiful ranch! It was the fanciest setup I had ever seen, and it smelled more like money than manure. He showed us their senior herd bull named Junior. I thought I was seeing two bulls in one hide. He told us Junior weighed 3240 pounds, at least a thousand pounds more than any bull I had ever seen.

The goats had to be unloaded, Mrs. Linam's bull loaded and tied securely in the front of the trailer, and the "chivos" reloaded in the back, before pulling out for home. U.S. Highway 290 was a two lane highway at that time and plenty busy. I have hauled lots of livestock, but that was probably the smartest bull I've ever hauled. Before we had gone two miles in heavy traffic, he'd figured out how to drive our pickup. He accomplished this by raising hell and throwing one fit after another causing the pickup and trailer to lurch from one side of the road to the other. His driving was not satisfactory, and I wondered if he was going to get us killed. Forty miles an hour was top speed, so I finally stopped and tied him a little tighter. This allowed us to share the driving responsibilities—he would drive half the time, and I would drive the rest. It took us five hours to get to Gatesville, only about 200 miles. There he finally quit driving and started riding.

I took the wheel, and we got home around 1:00 A.M. Monday morning. It had been one hard trip, but we had delivered the first load of buffalo; and believe me, the boys had plenty of stories to tell their friends at school on Monday.

I hauled several loads of the shaggy creatures and knew the supply was dwindling. I didn't realize how much until a San Antonio Insurance man called me to order eight or ten of them. I agreed to buy all I could and thought several were available. I bought the last three that Ty Field had for sale and put them in a pasture at my place while I looked for more.

One day I saddled up and drove the buffalo, some goats and cattle into a corral together to sort out the cattle. This is when I learned that buffalo, like some people, do not like goats. They look clumsy and awkward, but they are as quick as a cat. The third time the stinking old billy goat ran under a young buffalo bull, the bull whirled and butted the goat. He knocked him about ten feet and hit him twice more while he was rolling, then turned and kicked him in the side with both hind feet. This all took about five seconds and raised a knot on the Billy goat's side the size of a volley ball. I mentioned a smart bull earlier, but this goat was smart too, you couldn't drive him within twenty feet of a buffalo after that.

I scoured the entire area for a month looking for more buffalo, but to no avail. There were none to be had, so I called my customer to tell him I was ready to deliver the three that I had found. He stopped my heart for a few seconds when he said, "Dan, if three is all you can find, I'd as soon not fool with them."

I said, "Godamighty, Mr. Steen, I've bought and paid for these things and they're too damn tough to eat."

"Oh," he said, "I didn't know you had already bought them. Just bring what you have."

I started to breathe again. He gave me directions to his ranch south of Bandera, Texas, and we agreed that he would meet me there late the following Saturday afternoon.

David had begged to go with me on what I was sure would be the final trip, so I agreed. He asked another friend James Martin to come along this time.

As usual, we had trouble loading the Bison Buggy, so we arrived at the gate of the Steen Ranch just before sundown. A locked chain as big as my arm was stretched across the cattle guard so I knew Mr. Steen was gone. I was hot! I would have backed the trailer up to the gate and jumped the buffalo out into his pasture; but I had not been paid and I was afraid they would never be found in that rough country. We went back to Bandera, and I guess the Lord felt sorry for me. He performed one of His miracles by helping me to find someone who had a key to the gate. We put the three buffalo in a corral about 10:00 P.M. at the ranch and headed home.

I had a lump in my throat, realizing that the buffalo trading was over. There was no more demand and the supply was gone. It was the end of an era.

The State of Texas required that these animals, like cattle, had to be tested periodically for Brucellosis; and some ranchers, tired of the hassle, disposed of their herds. Others found that so-called "sportsmen" from Fort Worth, Dallas, or Houston would pay $3000.00 to shoot a big buffalo bull from a distance of fifty feet. Some fun, huh??

The business was good while it lasted; a different and somewhat exciting way to make a few dollars, but when the history book closes on the 1960s, I doubt seriously there will be anything said about "Dan Fields, The Last Of The Buffalo Traders."

Chapter 37

My First Plane Ride

Back in the latter part of the 1960's, among other things, I was operating a trucking business called State Line Trucks. In Texas at that time, the trucking business was regulated by the State Railroad Commission. As a Specialized Motor Carrier, my books were audited from time to time by a representative of the Commission. These guys were a real pain in my ass, but it was something I had to put up with. Until about 1970, I was able to outtalk these auditors; so they looked the other way a bit, and I was not subject to very much regulation at that time.

In 1970, the Commission sent a kid out from Austin, who was barely shaving. I found out pretty quick that he meant to get his name engraved in the granite of the Tribune Building in Austin, Texas, where the Railroad Commission's home office was located. He was a real, "sure enough, swaybacked, red roan horse's ass." He started auditing my books early one morning; and by 11:00 o'clock, he had written me up on every violation he could think of. I was getting a little warm under the collar by that time. He then started asking questions about a buy and sell business which I operated under—and in conjunction with the trucking business. This meant that I bought and sold grain, hay, and other commodities; adding the freight to the cost of the commodities. I told him that I did not believe this concerned him. He continued to ask questions.

I then told him, "I don't think this comes under the jurisdiction of the Railroad Commission."

He pressed on, so finally, in exasperation, I said, "Feller, I don't believe we're operating on the same wave length. There seems to be a breakdown in communication. You don't understand what I'm saying, so I'm going to change the way I say it. This is none of your damned business."

He understood that, and said, "I'm sorry, I didn't know you felt that way about it."

"That's exactly the way I feel about it!"

He thanked me, put his stuff in his briefcase and hit the road. I thought, "I wish I had told him that three hours ago."

A few days later I received a registered letter from the Railroad Commission, inviting me to come to Austin for a personal conference. I realized I was in serious trouble and certainly did not look forward to that meeting. I also knew that the young man I had told to mind his business was the reason for the letter.

I was managing a cotton gin at Higginbotham, Texas at the time. It was fall of the year and very difficult for me to leave the business for any length of time. My car was old and not very dependable, so I decided I would have to fly to Austin for the conference. That way I would only be gone for one day. I had flown in a small private plane a couple of times but had never flown commercially. I was, and still am, afraid of flying; but this seemed to be the logical way to go.

I made reservations to leave Lubbock at 7:30 a.m., and return on the same day at 5:30 p.m. This would give me several hours in Austin for the Railroad Commission to rake me over the coals.

I made the mistake of telling some of my customers about my plans. They knew about my fear of flying, so they had a field day. They teased me unmercifully and even made up a pot, which would go to the one who picked the nearest time of the crash of my plane. All this was not really as funny to me as it was to them. The night before I was to go to Austin, I set my alarm clock for 3:00 a.m. It was only a two-hour drive to Lubbock, but I wanted to have plenty of time to worry. I was as nervous as a long tailed tom cat in a room full of rocking chairs.

About 11:00 o'clock that night the telephone rang. It was my friend Jack McMillan. He said, "I've changed by mind. Instead of

$100,000 worth of flight insurance, I want you to buy a $200,000 policy in my name."

Very calmly I said, "You son-of-a-bitch, is that the only reason you called me?"

He said "Yes."

I said, "Thank you," and hung up.

He lived three quarters of a mile from me, but I'm sure I could hear him laughing after I hung up the phone.

When we took off from the Lubbock airport the next morning, I was cutting washers out of the seat an inch-and-a-quarter in diameter. You could say that I was uptight. I've run lots of machinery over the years, and I know that many times there is a warning before it fails, so I heard every noise the airplane made between Lubbock and Austin. The stewardess offered me some breakfast, but I was unable to eat. I did drink some coffee and a little juice, but mostly I was busy helping hold up the plane. We arrived in Austin on time, and a friend of mine named John Draper picked me up. He lobbied for the majority of the trucking business in Texas. This included what I referred to as the "poor boy truckers" such as myself. We went to his office where he gave me some advice on how to answer the questions the Railroad Commission people were going to ask me. We had lunch, and he dropped me off at the Tribune Building. I wondered if I would ever see my old friend again because I was sure they were going to hang me from the top of the building.

I met with Woody Walton, who was in charge of rates and auditing, and later with the Director Of Motor Transportation, Mr. Walter Wendlandt. They were very nice but also quite firm. They went over about fifty violations that the kid had written up on me, and explained that I was going to have to change the way I operated. The upshot of the meeting was that I was put on probation for eight months. This meant that if I was caught violating the regulations again, they would cancel my permit. It was worth a lot of money, and I could not afford for this to happen. I was most concerned about how I was going to be able to do business for the next eight months and still keep my nose as clean as they told me to. At the end of the probationary period, Woody was nice enough to help me figure a way out of this awful jam. He, his wife Sibyl, Joyce and I became close friends and visited each other until his death.

I caught a cab back to the airport; and while waiting for the plane, I ran into a friend of mine, Bruno Schroeder. He worked for the Texas Cooperatives but was on his way to Lubbock to referee a Texas Tech football game. When we got on the plane and took off, Bruno immediately went to sleep. I could not imagine anyone being able to sleep on an airplane. I could stay on one for two weeks and never close my eyes.

I was also sitting by an attorney from Tennessee who was a most interesting fellow. He had been Governor Clements' press secretary. He was telling me one joke or story after another, but I was having trouble concentrating on them. The pilot had headed the plane straight up, and I was sitting tight in the seat, as white as a sheet. It was a clear day, but we were so high I could hardly see the ground, and still climbing, when suddenly, the plane made a strange noise and the nose dropped sharply. That scared the fool out of me, but the lawyer continued to tell stories.

The second time the plane sputtered and the nose dropped, it was more pronounced. I jumped, and as I stuck my head up over the back of the seat, I saw several more heads looking around. At that time, my new friend from Tennessee had come to a point in his story where I was supposed to laugh or say something. When he gave me a questioning look, I turned to him and said, "Hell, feller, I don't have the slightest idea what you've been talking about. This damned airplane's fixin' to fall." I thought he would bust a gut laughing; and I'm quite sure, if he's still alive, he's got a good story about that country son-of-a-bitch from Higginbotham, Texas, that he rode with, coming out of Austin one day.

I was just as scared on the way home that afternoon as I had been that morning, but the difference was, I didn't have another meeting to attend, so when the stewardess came by my seat taking orders, I told her to bring me a drink, to make it a double, and to hurry. I had two more drinks before we got to Lubbock, and this stopped my knees from rattling. In fact, I was fortified enough to tell the stewardess she could sit on my lap and to ask the pilot if he would do a couple of slow rolls as we came into Lubbock. Brave as I felt, I know I was the happiest person on that plane to be back on the ground.

Chapter 38

Divine Intervention

My family and I were members of the First Methodist Church in Denver City, Texas, when Methodist preachers were still required to pay their own expenses when moving to a new church. I was in the trucking business, so I felt compelled to help with their moving, and especially since most of the ones I knew were not overpaid. Moving was fairly expensive, even at that time, so that was a small way that I could help. It would be hard for me to say that the Lord told me to do this; but as the scripture says, "He moves in strange ways."

As I recall, I moved several of them, some of whose names I do not remember; but I will relate to you a couple of moves which I thought were the more interesting ones.

We had a preacher once, who was just awful. People were leaving our church in droves, and some of us on the official board realized that something had to be done.

My banker friend, Red Tipps, called me rather late one night, and told me to pick up him and an attorney friend Paul New, at 6:00 o'clock the next morning.

I asked, "Why?"

He answered, "Annual Conference is going on in Amarillo, and we're going up there to get a new preacher. We'll be doing this on our own, since we are not delegates to the Conference. I hope we don't get kicked out of the church!"

The first thing we did when we got to Amarillo the next day was to talk to enough people to figure out that Davis Edens, the pastor at Wellington, Texas, was the man we wanted to hire. We found the delegates from our church, explained to them what our plans were, and they agreed.

The second thing we did was to locate Davis and see if he was interested in coming to Denver City as pastor. He indicated that he would be interested in moving, but would need more money than Denver City was paying the present preacher. Again, Red, Paul and I contacted the church delegates, but they did not have the authority to agree to pay him any more money. The three of us held a conference, and decided that Davis was definitely the man we wanted; and if our church refused to pay the several thousand dollars difference that he wanted, we would pay it ourselves.

Our next unusual act was to contact the Bishop and tell him what we had done. He nearly had a fit, and explained to us that this was highly unethical. He also stated that we should not have even talked to Davis, but talked to him instead and let him be the go-between. The Bishop was way too late, and we told him so. He was not a happy man.

The upshot of it was: we got Davis as our pastor and were very pleased about that. I agreed to go to Wellington and move him to Denver City.

I asked an old friend, Walt Ayers, who was retired, to go with me. Walt thought it was great to be able to make a trip in a big rig. When we got to Wellington about 10:00 o'clock on the given morning, the first thing I did was to pull in at a truck stop to fuel up.

Walt was paying close attention to the meter on the pump. It was spinning like the latch on an outhouse door. When it finally stopped on ninety gallons, Walt turned to me and asked, "How much fuel did you have in this thing when we left home?"

I told him, "It was full."

He said, "I'll never complain about my gas mileage again."

We found the Methodist parsonage and started to load up. The Edens had four children, and I've never seen as much stuff in my life. We filled a thirty-eight-foot trailer, and the last thing that had to go inside was one of those old-time, upright pianos. Joyce had one, so I knew it weighed a ton.

Davis was a genteel, soft-spoken, polite gentleman; so he turned as white as a sheet when I said, "Preacher, you'd better get the hell out of here." He couldn't imagine why; so I told him, "I've loaded a lot of these old pianos, and I've never been able to put one in a truck without cussing." He didn't know what to do; I was joshing him, but he didn't know it. He wrung his hands for a few minutes, gritted his teeth and hung on. We got the piano loaded without profanity, and the rest of the trip was uneventful.

The official board agreed to pay the amount we had offered Davis; so that saved the three of us quite a bit of money. I might add that the Edens family was a most delightful asset to our church and became some of our family's closest friends.

The next move I will tell about was moving Weldon McCormick and his family to Abilene, Texas. It was a great loss to our church; when they left, but again, I offered to move them, and they gratefully accepted.

I looked over the stuff that they had to move, and it was so little that instead of using one of my eighteen wheelers, I borrowed a bob-tail truck from my friend Jack McMillan. It would hold all their possessions and be much easier on their furniture. I picked up Jack's truck, took it to town to get an inspection sticker, and everything that could go wrong, went wrong. I spent a lot of money getting the truck ready, and I was sick of it.

Joyce's folks lived in Sweetwater, Texas, which was on the way to Abilene; so she and our children decided to ride down with me so we could spend a night with her mother and step-father Olin Dodson before I went on to Abilene. We loaded the truck, and my family and I headed for Sweetwater. We did not get very far down the highway until I got a signal from another truck driver that a State License and Weight Officer was down the road ahead of me. I could see a lot of things wrong with the truck, so I didn't look forward to running into a highway patrolman. I told the children, "Look, a patrolman is going to stop us in a few minutes, and regardless of what I tell him, you keep your mouths shut. The first one that says a word, gets it."

Fortunately, the patrolman had moved on before we got there.

A long way before we get to Sweetwater we could see a terrible cloud ahead of us; and there was no doubt but that we were going to get into a big rain. I had covered the truck with a tarp and was not too concerned, because I planned to put the truck in Joyce's step-dad's shop for the night.

By the time we got into Sweetwater, it was coming a cloudburst, and the rain was coming down in sheets. Joyce and the children got out at her mother's house while her step-dad and I went to the shop to put the truck inside, out of the rain. The truck was too big to go inside the door of the shop! I thought I might have a heart attack. I had those nice people's worldly possessions in the back of that truck, and I felt sure the tarp would not keep all the rain off their belongings. It was not a new tarp and was almost sure to leak.

I could find no other place in town where I could get the truck inside, so in desperation I parked it against the side of a big grocery store and went to bed. I slept very little that night and spent most of the night thinking about what I was going to do. I said lots of prayers.

I had several options:

1. I could take the truck to Abilene, park it in front of the house, jump out and run off.
2. Since the truck had a lift on the bed, I could back it into the front yard, raise the lift, dump all their possessions and drive away.
3. I could deliver their belongings to the house and face the music.

Of course, I chose the latter.

When I got to Abilene early the next morning, I pulled off the tarp; and we started unloading. I could not believe it, but nothing appeared to be damaged. Everything on that truck was dry. I found nothing that was wet except the last thing I carried off the truck. It was a portable typewriter, which had been covered by everything else. When I lifted it up, about ten drops of water ran out the bottom of the case.

I was pretty sure the Lord was saying to me, "Look, you knuckle head, you should have known that I would keep this preacher's precious things dry. Now do you believe in divine intervention?"

I most certainly do.

Chapter 39

Not Much of an Angel

What a bitch of a night, I thought, as I rolled south on an almost deserted Highway 62. Snow was whipped by a thirty-mile-an-hour north wind; and as I came through Brownfield, Texas, a few minutes earlier, a sign on the bank showed a temperature of 10 degrees at 3:00 A.M. I had not seen a bed in almost forty-eight hours; I was exhausted, but my mental computer told me I would be home in an hour. The big diesel engine in my eighteen-wheeler purred like a sick kitten as I pushed its rpm near the limit. Thank Heaven for a good heater!

Somewhere south of Wellman, Texas, through the snow, I saw a car without lights parked at the side of the highway. Suddenly, a man jumped out and frantically attempted to flag me down. Over the years I had helped dozens, maybe hundreds, of stranded motorists, but it had become increasingly dangerous. I was reluctant to stop for anyone; so as I rapidly approached the car, I wondered what to do. At the final instant the headlights of my truck flashed through the rear window of the car, my heart skipped a beat as I asked myself, "Could that have been a child's face in the window!" No more indecision—there was my answer; I started braking the big rig. Finding a place to turn around was not easy; but when I finally returned to the stalled automobile, the man ran to the door of my truck, and I could barely hear him above the throb of the diesel engine, as he yelled, "Thank God, you stopped! My wife and two children are in the car, and we are almost frozen! No one else even slowed down."

"Tell your family to get in the truck, it's warm in here," I said. "Then let's you and I try to start your car."

One of Dan's "big rigs," David and a couple of Dan's truck drivers.

We hooked up booster cables to crank the engine, but to no avail. While we were trying to start the stalled vehicle, he told me his name was Greene, he was a CPA, and lived in Seminole, Texas. He and his family were returning from a holiday when suddenly their car died, and the lights went out. After a number of futile attempts, we finally decided the car would not start. He asked, "What in the world am I going to do? Can you send a wrecker?"

"No, we'll leave your car here, and I'll take you home," I replied.

He asked, "Will all of us fit in the cab of your truck?"

"Sure we will," I said. "We don't have a choice."

We were plenty crowded with him, his wife, a five-year-old girl, a seven-year-old boy, and me in the cab of the truck, but they were so happy to be warm again. For the children, it almost became a festive occasion, as I let each of them honk the loud air horn and help me apply the trailer brakes. The family was delivered safely home, in Seminole; and they were so grateful that it was hard for me to get away from them. They wanted to make coffee, feed me, and pay me—all of which I declined. I just wanted to go home.

The snow was falling harder by the time I headed for home, but there was a warm feeling in the cab that had not been there before.

I had driven a good many miles out of my way in the storm, but I knew I had done my good deed for the day.

Several days later, my wife Joyce brought a package from the Post Office and asked, "Who do you know in Seminole named Greene who would send a package to you?"

For a moment I didn't know——then remembered the stranded family. As I unwrapped the package, I told Joyce what had happened. She was so proud of me. I took the lid off the box, and what a surprise to find a set of six, beautiful coffee mugs and a note beginning with, "To an Angel of Mercy." It went on to say that I had saved their lives, and a lot of other stuff which was not exactly true; but it surely made good reading!

I sent a note to the Greenes, which said, "Thank you for the beautiful coffee mugs. I appreciate them very much, but I appreciate, even more, being called an "Angel of Mercy." I've never, before, been called an angel of any kind!

Chapter 40

Sir!

The sun was low in the western sky as I steered the old blue Roadmaster Buick onto a remote strip of highway known as Telephone Road. This road, which stretches from the Midland airport to Seminole, Texas, is traveled only by oil field workers and a few ranchers. It goes through the dead center of nowhere.

As I turned north, the sun hit me in the side of the head, so I removed my radar detector from the sun visor and handed it to my wife, Joyce. I pulled the sunshade down and poured the coal to "old blue." My thoughts were of home at the "Higginbotham Hacienda" some sixty miles away. I was still picking up speed, when I rounded a slight curve and suddenly saw a State Highway Patrol car coming from the opposite direction at a distance of about one hundred yards.

"Oh hell," I said, "I've just got myself a ticket!" I was right—red lights came on just at that time.

It took a while for me to stop and longer for the patrolman to turn around and catch up with me. I was waiting outside my car when he came roaring up and jumped out of his car. As he approached me, I made a quick assessment of his personality. I decided he was not a nice man, and he was hot under the collar.

When I handed him my driver's license, I chuckled to myself as I considered showing him my Gaines County "Special Deputy" card which Sheriff V.A. Harris had given to both Joyce and me. It was an honorary title, but one which few people could brag about. I quickly decided that he was not in the mood for jokes. I also noted that he did not immediately return my license. That was not a good sign.

Angrily, he asked, "Any reason for you to be flying so close to the ground?"

The best reply I could come up with was, "Yes, sir, I was trying to get home."

Apparently that was not a valid reason.

The patrolman's voice was shaking when he said, "I clocked you at seventy-nine miles an hour in a fifty-five mile an hour zone!"

Pleasantly, I replied, "Well, sir, I've never been down this road doing less than eighty. Maybe my problem was driving too slow."

That was not a good answer. It started a lot of heated conversation, and at one point I wondered if he might draw his pistol. He finally, and very reluctantly, handed back my license with a citation which contained several comments regarding speed and attitude. I hoped the son-of-a-bitch's dog bit him when he got home.

As I climbed back into "old blue" and headed up the road once more, I asked, "Joyce, did you see that damned cop?"

"No," she said, "But I told you three times that the radar detector was squawking."

I hadn't heard a word she had said, but sure enough, the detector light was flashing, and it was still sounding off. I had literally been lost in thought.

I didn't learn much of a lesson from this experience, but I did wonder if I should have said "Sir" three times instead of twice.

Chapter 41

The Squirrely Suction Feeder

One cold, dreary morning in 1976, we were about caught up at the gin because of wet weather. I was home alone, so I decided to reward myself. We usually did not receive the Sunday newspaper until Monday afternoon around 4:00 or 5:00 o'clock. That particular day I decided to drive to Denver City, Texas, a distance of fifteen miles, to pick up a newspaper while it was still news. The weather was cold, and a light rain was falling.

About a mile north of the gin, I noticed an old pickup pulled over on the side of the road with the hood up. A couple of men appeared to be trying to start it, and several small children were around; so I stopped and asked what the problem was. The younger man, named Gilbert, answered, "We no gotee some gas." As usual, I had a can of gas with me, so I poured some in their pickup and told them to start it.

Gilbert replied, "We don't got no starter neither."

I thought he meant their battery was dead, but he raised the hood and showed me an empty hole in the flywheel cover where a starter would normally fit.

Dumbfounded, I asked, "Where in the world are you going on this cold morning with no gas and no starter?"

Gilbert, who was the the spokesman for the family, answered, "We're going to that gin down there," pointing toward the gin which I managed.

"What are you going to do there," I asked.

"We going to get a job."

"Do you know anyone there?"

"No."

"How do you know they'll hire you?"

"Oh, they hire us."

"Do you have any money?"

"No."

I helped them push the pickup and told them to follow me. I took them down to the gin, gave them a house where they could get warm, then took the father to town, bought them some groceries, and told the two men to come to work the next morning at 7:00 o'clock.

I realized I had not hired a couple of geniuses; but they appeared to be fit for work, and I knew they needed a job. I also knew they did not have a nickel to their name.

When Joyce came home that evening, I told her about the family and their circumstances. She gathered up a few clothes for the children, and reluctantly included a favorite floral sweater of hers for the mother. When they came to work the next morning, Gilbert's dad was wearing Joyce's flowered sweater! I could hardly keep from laughing, because I knew Joyce would be fighting mad when she saw him in the sweater.

I started them out feeding the suction, which is a large, movable pipe that feeds cotton into the gin. We were not very busy at the time so I thought it would give them a chance to learn their new job. They did not seem to be working very hard, but I hoped they would improve with a little time. However, as time went by and we began to get busier, they did not seem to be doing any better. I suspected that the father might be telling Gilbert not to work very hard.

A few days passed, and suddenly we were covered up with cotton. It was time for everyone on the place to "turn it on." Gilbert and his father were still not doing a very good job, so one morning I climbed up into the trailer with them, and explained that we sure as hell couldn't gin the cotton if they didn't get it into the gin. They continued to "dog around," so I fired them both.

Sometime later that morning I went out to Freeman's grocery, which was about 300 yards from the gin to pick up some bolts. Gilbert, his

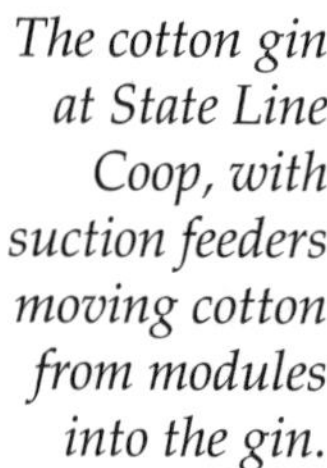

The cotton gin at State Line Coop, with suction feeders moving cotton from modules into the gin.

mother, and several of the small children were inside the store cashing their checks. I felt terrible for them because I knew they needed the job, so I told the mother that I was sorry about what had happened. She said that her husband was not well, and really not able to work, but Gilbert could work, and if given another chance, would do so.

I reluctantly said, "Gilbert, if you really want to work, you get your ass back out to that gin, but I want to see that suction pipe moving, and I don't mean maybe." He hit the door in a trot.

I picked up my bolts and started back to the gin, but when I got outside the store, my pickup was gone. I couldn't imagine what had happened until I finally looked toward the gin and saw it parked in front of the building. I quickly realized what had happened. That silly assed Gilbert had driven my pickup back to the gin and left me afoot. I thought I might fire him again, but I just walked back to the gin, madder than a wet hen, and read the riot act to him.

A few days later, I was looking out the office window and saw Gilbert coming toward the office in a hurry. As he got closer, I noticed a lump and a bruise on his jaw. Any time he started to tell me something, he would say, "Dan, I got to tell you something," and then proceed with what he wanted to say.

He came through the door and said, "Dan, I got to tell you something. I got to quit."

"Why," I asked?

"Mike, the truck driver hit me."

"Why did Mike hit you?

"He a'cuse me of eating his lunch."

"Well, did you eat it?"

"I chos ate wan!" (whatever that meant).

"You don't need to quit, just get your ass back out to the gin; don't eat Mike's lunch anymore, and he won't hit you anymore." Gilbert slowly returned to work.

A few mornings later, when I arrived at the gin about 6:00 o'clock in the morning, it was as cold as the mischief. As I walked through the door of the building I saw the hands digging cotton out of machinery all over the gin. It was choked from one end to the other. Everyone was busy except Gilbert, who was sitting on his ass on a three legged stool, warming his feet by the heater.

As I passed by where he was sitting, I said, "Gilbert, get your ass off that stool and get to work!"

I went on through the gin to check on everything and in a few minutes returned to the front of the building where the heater was located. There sat Gilbert on the stool, still warming his feet.

Upset, I yelled, "Gilbert, I told you to get your ass off that stool and get to work!"

Calmly, Gilbert replied, "I don't work here no more."

I said, "If you don't work here no more, then get the hell out of here. You're not going to sit around here while everyone else is working!"

"I stay here 'til I get my sheck," He announced.

My voice lowered about two octaves as I said slowly and carefully, "No, Gilbert, your gonna' stay around here until you get another damned knot on the side of your head." I was doubling up my right fist as I said it.

Gilbert suddenly realized what was about to happen to him and hauled ass. The last I ever saw of him was the soles of his tenny shoes as he went out the door in a dead run.

Chapter 42

The Flying Mexican

From the late 1940's until the early 1960's, farmers and ranchers were able to contract Mexican Nationals, called braceros, to work on farms and ranches.

My neighbor Albert had farmed south of McCamey, Texas, before moving to Higginbotham; and one year he contracted about thirty braceros to pick cotton. One Saturday afternoon his foreman took them to the local beer joint for some recreation, and they really got "beered up." They were in the back of an old truck; and on the way home, one Pepe Garcia shouted to his friends, "Watch me fly!!" Flapping his arms wildly, he dove out of the back of the truck, landed on his head, which broke his neck and killed him dead as a doorknob.

After a lengthy investigation by the Justice of the Peace, the Sheriff's Office and the Mexican Consulate, the body was turned over to Albert.

Albert was a fine man who wanted to do the right thing; so, at his own expense, he had Pepe embalmed and put in a cheap coffin for transportation back to the Bracero Contracting Center at Eagle Pass, Texas. The undertaker didn't finish with the body until about 10:00 o'clock that night. Albert's neighbor Marshall Marshall decided to go with him in case he needed help. By the time they loaded the coffin into the back of Albert's pickup, it was late when they left McCamey.

They were driving down the highway at 2:00 or 3:00 o'clock in the morning when suddenly they heard three loud knocks on the top of the pickup.

Marshall hollered, "Goddamn, Albert! That Mexican has come alive!"

It scared the fool out of both of them, and they spent the rest of the trip listening for "Pepe," but all was quiet.

When they got to Eagle Pass early the next morning, nobody on either side of the border wanted to take the body. The American government didn't want him, and neither did the Mexicans.

They hauled him all over Eagle Pass in the back of the pickup for most of the day. They had to call back to McCamey and have a death certificate wired to Eagle Pass, they had to provide a birth certificate from his home town in Mexico and all kinds of other paperwork had to be filled out. Finally, late that afternoon, the Mexican Consul agreed to take possession of the body.

Albert was as comical as anyone I ever knew, and when he got excited his eyes bugged out. As he told me this story, his eyes almost popped out of their sockets; but he didn't smile when he said, "If I ever get another one of those bastards killed, I'm going to put him in a cotton sack, haul him to Eagle Pass, and shake the son of a bitch out of the sack right in the middle of the International Bridge."

Chapter 43

Cow Chip Champ

One morning, many years ago, a bunch of my friends and I were sitting around my office at the gin, having a very good bull session. A neighbor from just across the New Mexico state line came in and made what we considered to be a rather "crappy" announcement:

He said, "My name is Ritter Holder, and I'm the New Mexico State Champion Cow Chip Thrower."

Now, I had chunked a few cow turds as a boy, (well selected cow turds, I might say); but a contest for this? Ridiculous! I never heard of one! However, two or three months later, one of the friends came in with a very small, four or five line, announcement which he had clipped out of a magazine, stating that the World Champion Cow Chip Throwing Contest would soon be held in Beaver, Oklahoma. That was too good to pass up. Ritter and I enjoyed pulling pranks and playing tricks on each other, so I thought this over and decided: "Man, I gotta' do something about this!"

I sat down, and with tongue in cheek, penned the following letter to the Chamber of Commerce in Beaver:

March 24, 1972
Chamber of CommerceBeaver, Oklahoma 73932

Gentlemen:

In reading the April-May issue of the American Farmer, I find that on April 22, 1972, you are sponsoring the World Champion Cow Chip Throwing Contest. One of my neighbors, who lives across the state line in New Mexico has stated that he is the New

Mexico State Champion Cow Chip Thrower, and I would like to pose the following questions:

1. Is this event sanctioned by the APCCT (Association of Professional Cow Chip Throwers), or is it just an amateur show?
2. If it is a sanctioned event, why has the New Mexico State Champion, Mr. Ritter Holder, East Star Rt., Lovington, New Mexico not been invited?
3. If this contest is not recognized by APCCT, what rules are to be used?

Mr. Holder has been in a rage since learning of this meet and declares that he would not participate if invited. He is also making very derogatory remarks concerning Oklahoma in general and Beaver in particular. I have tried to explain that his invitation was either lost in the mail, or it was a mere over-sight on your part.

I would consider it a favor if you could send him an invitation and I will do my best to soothe his injured feelings. If he could be persuaded to appear, it would certainly be a boost to your contest, as he has one of the largest galleries in the country.

If you are able to comply with this request, please include a set of rules regarding entrance fee, dimensions, moisture content and whether chips are furnished by you or the contestant.

Please advise me as soon as possible so this serious matter can be resolved without further hard feelings between New Mexico and Oklahoma.

Very truly yours,

RITTER HOLDER FAN CLUB
Dan Fields, President
P.O. Box 836
Denver City, Texas 79323

DF/y
cc: Mr. Hoyt Caldwell
%KLEA Radio Station
Lovington, New Mexico

I did not have a typewriter available, so I took it to a friend in the bank in Denver City, Texas, and asked her to type it for me. She read the letter, chuckled, and said, "This is a bunch of shit!"

When she had typed the letter, I hurried to the post office and mailed it to Beaver, Oklahoma.

A few days later, I received the following letter from the Chamber of Commerce in Beaver. I could not believe they thought I was serious, but maybe they did.

March 26, 1972

Mr. Dan Fields, President
Ritter Holder Fan Club
P.O. Box 836
Denver City, Texas 79323

Dear President Fields:

Mistaken identity. I have been sending all those communications to Denver, Colorado.

In the correspondence I have had with K.D.E.F., Albuquerque, N.M., a Mr. Dan Evans failed to mention anything about Assn. of PCCT, in fact, he suggested that they would sponsor any man or woman with a good reputation, physical stamina and average capabilities to represent New Mexico, in the WORLD CHAMPIONSHIP COW CHIP THROWING CONTEST, HELD IN BEAVER, OKLAHOMA April 22,1972, which is the third annual contest.

I am truly sorry of this oversight. By the way, where is Denver City, Texas and Lovington, N.M.?

We have been contacted by some one who claimed to represent an organization and I think he did mention something about Association of Professional Cow Chip Throwers. I'm sorry about that for I did not read all of the letter. I actually thought it was a crank and I filed his letter in file 13.

Of course as you read the rules, which I have enclosed, you will see that only "Champions" of Sanctioned Regional Contests will be assured of a chance to enter, and none, regardless of his prominence, will be entered after the dead line of April 8th, 1972 (or when we will reach 50 entrees in any one class. The men and women's open is the one last to fill.)

You still have time to make it, and I assure you that we would like for you fellows to participate, so get old Ritter Holder mentally subdued and in training and get his managers on the ball and we will see you at the show.

Be here for Saturday morning as we have a real good parade and free barbecue at noon. We are so crowded for time if you will forgive this time, I will consider this letter to the whole group involved in the consoling of the "Champ," an invitation to our spring Celebration. It was nice to hear from you.

Sincerely yours,

Beaver Chamber of Commerce
Ralph Procter, Secy-mgr

They had sent a copy of their letter to Ritter. Now, as a rule, he had a wonderful sense of humor; but somehow, he never thought it was as funny as the rest of us did. I had sent a copy of my letter to his friend who managed the radio station in Lovington, New Mexico. I felt sure he would read this letter on the air, during his morning news program. I think, until this day, that Ritter threatened him with bodily harm if he aired it. The letter was never read on the radio.

Before time for this contest in Oklahoma came up, Ritter came by the office several times; and each time, I begged him to make the trip with me to Beaver. I said, "Ritter, I want you to go to Beaver, Oklahoma. With me; it won't cost you a nickel. I'll pay all the expenses. You can win this contest, Ritter! As big and strong as you are, the other folks won't have a chance. We'll go up on Friday. Now, on Friday night you'll have to stay in training; but picture this: on Saturday, when you heave the last cow turd, with the roar of the crowd in your ears, the smell of victory (or something) in your nostrils, and they hang that gold plated cow turd around your neck, I'll be standing right behind you with a quart of that old Oklahoma corn whiskey. I'll wine you and dine you; nothing will be too good for you. You will be the best treated man in Western Oklahoma. You've got to go!!"

The only response I ever got from Ritter was: "You little bastard, you gotta' be kiddin'!"

CHAPTER 44

Best Damn Cotton Ginner in Texas Award

My wife Joyce and I were headed east on Interstate 10. Spring was in the air and we were glad to get away from the cold, dry, sandy plains of Gaines County, Texas. Five or six weeks before, in early 1989, we had finished ginning a record crop at State Line Coop Gin and were ready for some rest and relaxation.

We were going to Arlington, Texas for the joint annual meeting of the Texas Agricultural Cooperative Council and the Texas Bank for Cooperatives. This was a state-wide meeting of cooperatives of all kinds: cotton gins, grain elevators, supply stores, telephone, electrical and bank cooperatives, which constituted a rather large gathering. We looked forward to this event from year to year.

As we rolled down the highway, I was sipping my third cool beer and reflecting on what a successful, intelligent, debonair, suave gentleman I was.

I thought to myself, "This beer sure makes me feel prosperous. Well, not so rich; I just don't mind being poor so damn bad!"

I had the world in my hand; the world was an oyster, and I was the pearl. As we traveled east, I watched the country green up and saw the flowers were starting to bloom. We always enjoyed coming to this part of the country in the spring of the year.

Joyce asked me if I had any particular duties to attend to at the meeting this year; and my answer was, "Yes, John Barnes is receiving a very important award; and since it's a surprise, my job is to deliver him to the meeting on Friday afternoon."

John was my very good friend who worked for Plains Coop Oil Mill in Lubbock. He and I were inclined to skip some of the business meetings. During previous meetings, when we got tired and bored, we slipped out to do something different, but his award was to be presented around 2:30 o'clock Friday afternoon, and I was supposed to be sure he was there to receive it.

The meeting started on Thursday and nothing eventful happened that day. On Friday morning, J. R. Bloomrosen, an attorney friend of mine, was presented with an award from the Texas Bank for Cooperatives.This was one of four awards presented at each annual meeting.

At noon, John and I went to lunch; and when we finished eating, John announced, "I'm not going back to that damn meeting this afternoon."

I had to do something; so I said, "Well, John, I'm gonna' go. If the Board of Directors is good enough to pay my way down here and pay me while I'm here, the least I can do is attend the meetings." I was intentionally shaming him a little bit.

After thinking a minute or two, he said, "Well, I'll go with you."

So back to the meeting we went. The speaker was the worst I've ever heard in my life, and he talked for an hour or more. I thought I was going to have to hold John, but we finally got through it, and John was presented with the Distinguished Service Award, which he certainly deserved. He was most pleased, and so was I. I had done my job.

In those days, several of my closest friends and I played a little poker when there was a break in the meetings. John and I felt it was our duty to teach the younger fellows how to play. That day was no exception. I had left a note for Joyce, telling her what room I would be in if she needed me. The game was in full swing, about 4: 30 P.M. When the phone rang. Someone answered and said, "Dan, that was Joyce, and she said the banquet starts at 6:30. She also said for you to be in your room at 5:00 o'clock, and she didn't mean five after five."

That was completely out of character for her. I mumbled, "I'll go when I get ready."

As you might suspect, I sauntered into our hotel room about five minutes after five and picked up the ice bucket. I thought I might have a little George Dickel before dinner.

Joyce said, "Have you been drinking?"

I answered, "No."

"Are you sure?"

"Hell, yes, I'm positive!"

"Didn't they have anything to drink at the poker game?"

"I guess they did, I didn't notice. What the hell's the matter with you, anyway?"

That was not at all like her, and later we laughed about all the questions.

The highlight of the convention was the annual presentation of the two most coveted, prestigious state awards. They were to be presented during the banquet. One was "Cooperative Ginner of the Year" chosen from cotton gin managers across the state. The other was "Cooperator of the Year," usually selected from one of the larger regional cooperatives. Joyce had learned that another good friend, Wayne Martin, was to receive the latter. Only the immediate family of the recipient and a few very close friends knew who it would be. Joyce had been helping his wife, Eugenia, keep his family out of sight until the proper time when they would be introduced at the banquet. Joyce also told me that we were to go early to seat Wayne and his wife at a table near the podium and keep them there. I told her that Wayne could get to the front by himself, that I was not going early. We went early!

The banquet hall was full, and we watched as a very surprised Wayne Martin was named "Cooperator of the Year." He was completely "taken aback" when his family stood to be introduced.

Bob Newton, another dear friend of mine, was introduced to pay tribute to and announce the "Ginner of the Year." He talked at length about the importance of this award. He mentioned that it was presented to a man judged to have rendered the greatest service to his patrons, his community and the cotton industry in general, etc., etc., etc. I was sitting there thinking, "Man, I wish he'd get to it, and we'd get this thing over with so we could get on about our business—we might even have another poker game if Joyce doesn't have plans."

Suddenly, I heard the Master of Ceremonies say, "The Board President of this year's award winner told me that in 1969, this man became general manager of their gin, which was flat broke. He started his career with a wornout, four-bale-an-hour plant."

I thought, "Damn, that's when I started."

The speaker continued, "Because of his tenacity, hard-nosed will and good-humored spunk, our gin made it. In 1973, he moved a better gin to our community."

At this, I leaned over to Joyce and whispered, "Joyce, could he be talking about me?" Oh, she looked so smug and proud!

As he continued, I was becoming more and more suspicious, but I couldn't believe it. I never in my wildest dreams thought I would be considered for this prestigious award. Some cotton ginners called it "The Best Damn Ginner In Texas" award. But, when he finally said, "He has been a member of the Denver City First United Methodist Church for thirty-six years, I whispered again, "Joyce, he's talking about me!" And, sure enough, he was!!

So many undeserving, nice things were said. I didn't believe them, but they sure sounded good. Finally, I was invited to come to the podium to speak. At that time, I saw my children, grandchildren, other family members, my Board of Directors and their wives standing to be introduced. They had come from New Mexico, New Orleans and a lot of places in between. Talking is easy for me, but at that moment it was one of the most difficult things I have ever done. It was a very emotional time for me. The Ginner of the Year Award selection, made by my peers, was the highest honor I had ever received. It was the proudest moment of my life.

Joyce, the family and a few friends had known about it for almost

Dan is awarded the prestigious "Ginner of the Year Award" by Bob Newton.

a year, but I never suspected it could happen to me. As you might guess, Wayne Martin had been instructed to get me to the banquet and keep me there. His wife had also helped Joyce hide our family at the hotel!

At the reception for Wayne and me in the ballroom, following the banquet, Joyce finally told me and the family why she was quizzing me about drinking earlier that day. She explained, "I knew you were going to have to make remarks at the banquet, and I didn't want you getting up there, slurring," Duh, duh, duh!"

What an unbelievable occurrence. Three of my closet friends and I had won all four of the coveted state-wide awards. That would never happen again in a thousand years!!

Plaque given to the
"Best Damn Ginner of the Year."

Chapter 45

Tribute to John Barnes

This is a silly poem I wrote and read to my very good friend, John Barnes, at his retirement party in December, 1988. It is only the third poem I have ever written; the first two being the one Bargy and I wrote at the Lloyd Mountain School (see story called "Pee & Poetry), and the other for my son-in-law, Robert Dewlen, when he graduated from college (see story called "Hangin' On and Hangin' In").

There once was a fellow named Barnes,
who grew up on East Texas farms.
He taught FFA,
and thought it O.K.,
but was called off to war to bear arms.

He later hired on with Murray,
who fired his ass in a hurry.
He started to toil
at Lamesa Cotton Oil,
then came back to Lubbock to worry.

He then worked for a fellow named Herzer,
who told him, "Most gins need a merger."
Now his task went fine
'til he went to State Line
and learned that his nice days got worser.

For there was a nice man named Dan,
who said, "Fix my gin? Yes, you can."
Dan spoke in a whisper,
and always said, "Mister,"
and never said, "Change that damn plan!"

Now, back to the Oil Mill came John.
The war at State Line, he had won.
He came home in glory.
That's the end of this story.
At State Line he had hit a home run.

Now the Oil Mill provided his dough,
but the gins were the winner, you know!
He made them all money,
called the bookkeepers "Honey",
with ginners he's the only all Pro!!

PART V

Laughing, Loving, and Death

Chapter 46

Friendly Foolishness

Jack McMillan and I have been friends for more than 50 years. During that period we have pulled many pranks on each other. I will only attempt to tell about a few of them.

I suppose some of this foolishness started one day when Jack had pulled his eighteen-wheeler into the narrow driveway between the two cotton gins, where I worked in Higginbotham, Texas. Jack was sitting in his truck waiting for the gin hands to unload the bagging and ties that he had delivered. Both gin plants were running; there was a tremendous amount of noise. I had a lot on my mind and was completely oblivious to what was going on. I walked across the driveway, not realizing there was a truck within a mile of me. Jack waited until I was in the dead center of the truck then pulled the chain on the air horn. I was so far away in never-never land, that I did not know but what I was in the middle of a major highway when the horn blared. The noise was so loud and scared me so badly that I thought I was trying to run, but when Jack got through laughing, he said, "You looked just like a big-assed bird; you humped up and froze." I knew my heart was OK, or I would have had an attack at that very moment.

I repaid him for that! I got into the back seat of his car one night after dark, and, as he drove across the gin yard, I stuck the neck of a Coca Cola bottle to the back of his neck and said, "Stick 'em up, you son of a bitch." I don't suppose anyone ever got into a car in the darkness without thinking about the fact that someone could be in the back seat. That scared him almost as badly as the truck horn incident had scared me. He told me that the bottle really felt like cold steel on his neck.

Once when Jack was helping me haul cottonseed, he sent word to me by his truck driver, that he had knocked a big hole in the seed house wall, and that I should tell ole' Fuzz (Jack's pet name for the guy who was serving as gin manager at that time) that if he wanted to see him he would be at Dan's Bar. Of course, that was a big lie, he had not damaged the seed house. Jack thought it was hilarious, but it caused some serious problems between the manager and me. However, I figured out how to turn the tables on Mr. McMillan!

I told him, "Jack, I need you to move some more cottonseed, because my insurance adjuster from Lubbock couldn't find the hole in the seed house, and he is coming back tomorrow."

Jack looked like the chickens had run over him and sheepishly said, "Dan, you know I didn't knock a hole in that building. I was running the loader myself—I was just teasing you! You didn't REALLY call the adjuster, did you?"

I said, "Why in the hell shouldn't I have called him? You said the building was damaged. Boy, ole' Fuzz, and the adjuster are going to think this is the funniest thing they've ever heard."

Jack just looked sick, so I let him sweat until late that afternoon, when I finally admitted to him, "I was just teasing you, I didn't REALLY call the insurance man."

Such bits of foolishness went on for many years, with neither of us getting much ahead of the other, but the last one (at least I hope to hell it was the last) was the best.

Jack was the best neighbor anybody ever had, as well as a very close friend. We worked together, played together, and occasionally drank a little beer together. He was a bachelor until he was in his forties, so he showed up at our house at meal times fairly often. He was always welcome. We enjoyed his visits, and our three children adored him. Jack was the kind of neighbor who was hard to do anything for, since he did most of the giving. However, several years later, after he was married, his trailer house burned; and he and his family came to live with us for a while. We were so glad to get to pay him back in a small way for all the nice things he had done for us.

He was a very close mouthed fellow, and I was probably the only person in the country who knew anything about his business before he married. He was always bringing things to our family, so one day when he said, "Old man Rawlings has six or seven sows for sale. What do you think about me buying them?"

I told him, "I think that's a fine idea." The reason I thought it was such a fine idea was that I knew we would be receiving some hog meat.

Jack bought the sows, and when they started having pigs, several of them had only one or two. He was certainly not a person to discuss his business in public, so I liked to wait until the gin office was full of people and ask, "Jack, how many pigs did that sow have?" He would turn as red as a beet and mumble, "One" or "Two," whichever the case happened to be. The reason that was such a source of amusement to me, was simply because it made him so damned mad; so when two are three of them had several pigs, I stopped asking him about them.

Needless to say, the hog business was a sore subject with Jack.

Jack had bought a new trailer house, and one day while I was passing, a crew was setting up the trailer. An old sow was standing out in the yard carefully watching as they blocked up the trailer. I was inspired! The first time Jack came by the office when it was full of people, I asked "Jack what are you going to do about all those damn hogs getting under your trailer?"

I realized immediately that I had drawn blood. It made Jack so mad he didn't know what to do. He testily replied, "There'll be no damned hogs under my trailer."

I said, "Sure there will be. It'll be cool, and there'll be a few water leaks, so they'll probably stay under there all the time. It seems to me though, that it will be hard to take a nap in the afternoon with all those damned hogs rubbing on the bottom of the trailer and squealing."

He was beginning to get a little white around the ears when he snapped, "Goddammit, I told you there won't be any hogs under my trailer!"

I continued to fan the fire regarding the hog business for several days. Then one day some "knuckle head" announced that he thought we should have a house warming for Jack's new trailer. Several of us planned this get-together; and since Jack was still a bachelor, we invited only the men in the community. It figured to be the social event of the year at Higginbotham.

On the day of the to-do, I got our son David and one of our hired hands to help me with a fun project. I had brought along a tape recorder and had them catch a hog and hold him by the ears so he would really squeal while I caught all of that racket on tape. David told me later that he was pretty sure the tape would sell.

Time came for the big party. I purposely arrived late, knowing all the other guests were there. Before going in, I turned the tape player on with the volume as high as it would go and placed it under the step. I had left the first few minutes of the tape silent, to give me time to get into the house and sit down in the living room.

Jack was in the kitchen fixing drinks, and I was watching him carefully. Suddenly the most ungodly squealing commenced from underneath the trailer. It sounded exactly like a hog was pinned beneath it. Everyone had a look of disbelief on their faces as though they wondered what they were going to do about the squealing pig. Jack did not look like he was moving very fast, but he was at the front door in an instant and opened it slightly, as though he thought the hog might come inside. He had what I called a "community dog" named Max: which he carried around in the back of his pickup. As he opened the door slightly, he said, "Sic 'em, Max!" I lost my breath laughing. He told me later, "Max was smarter than I was; he stared at the porch and cocked his head from side to side."

It took a few seconds for Jack to figure out what had happened, but he finally ran outside, looked under the step and brought the tape recorder inside. It was still squealing wildly. He said, "Dan Fields, you son of a bitch."

By that time everyone had realized that this was a joke and were laughing uncontrollably. I was in hysterics. I don't believe that I have ever been as tickled in my life.

Two fellows in the community had come together, one a religious man and one who "said he was." Suddenly, Forrest, the religious one, said, "Come on, Lewis, we'd better go, these guys are fixin' to have some fun."

They hadn't stepped off the porch before somebody hollered, "Where's that goddammed whisky?"

Jack told me later that for a long time people he didn't even know approached him on the street in town to ask him if he was the "hog man." Jack and I had pulled so many pranks on each other that I looked over my shoulder for several years after this incident; but now after many, many years, I really think we're through with our foolishness. I hope!

Chapter 47

The Reverend McMillan

Several years ago, my good friend Jack McMillan, his son Mike, my son David, two more of our friends from Higginbotham, and I attended a morning funeral in Carlsbad, New Mexico. After the funeral, the six of us went to the Stephens Hotel Restaurant, there in Carlsbad for lunch. As the hostess started to seat us, she paused momentarily and said, "Oh no, I forgot. There's a preachers' meeting in here, I'll need to put you in another room."

I replied, "Goodness, no, don't put us with any preachers"; and pointing to Jack, I said, "This man is a Church of Christ minister, himself, but we are just passing through town and would like some privacy."

Cheerfully, the hostess said, "My, isn't that nice; I'm Church of Christ, myself. Where is your church located?"

Now, Jack was anything but a preacher; so embarrassed and a bit rattled, Jack blurted out, "Bottomhicky!" instead of Higginbotham.

The hostess blushed and said, "Uh, that's nice, but I don't believe I know where that is."

After she seated us, the waitress took our orders; and everyone but Jack and I decided to go through the buffet line. He and I ordered a sandwich and a beer. I noticed that every time the hostess came through the room she glared at Jack and me and the beer sitting in front of us on the table. I was certain that she would be asking our waitress a lot of questions about the "beer drinking preachers;" so I thought I would help her day a bit.

We finished eating; and as the waitress was preparing our check I knew she was listening to every word we said, so I casually mentioned to the other fellows, "I certainly hope the Elders of the Church never find out that we like beer. We don't have a chance to have one very often; but when we're in a place where no one knows us, it's always good to have a couple."

She was still "all ears"; so as she handed us our check, I said to Jack, "Reverend McMillan, hurry up and finish your beer; we need to be on the road. We have that revival meeting starting in Kansas tomorrow night, and we are going to have to hurry to make it on time."

As we walked out the door, I heard the waitress tell the hostess, "Wait 'til your preacher hears about this!"

Chapter 48

The Loose Tooth

When I was just a kid, I was leaning forward in the saddle, when suddenly my horse threw his head back, smacking me in the mouth. My two upper front teeth were almost knocked out; and several years later, after Joyce and I were married, one of them turned dark. Then one morning, I woke up with an awful ache in a lower front tooth. I went to see the cheapest dentist in Colorado City, Texas; hoping he would rub some sort of soothing balm on it. He was out of soothing balm. He looked in my mouth and exclaimed, "The nerve in that upper front tooth is dying. That's your problem; it'll have to come out!"

I said, "Hell, Doc, it's my lower tooth that hurts."

"No, that's a sympathetic pain from the upper one."

"Pull it," I said. He did!

Joyce and I had been married for a couple of years, and she must have still thought I was good looking, because she took one look at the blank space in my mouth and started crying. My lower tooth continued to hurt; so later in the day, I returned to the dentist's office and said, "Dammit, Doc, you pulled the wrong tooth!"

"My, my,"he said, "It must be the lower one."

I snapped, "You'd better be right this time, if you know what's good for you!"

He pulled the lower tooth, and the pain stopped.

Later he plugged up the hole where my upper tooth had been with what he called a "thumb plate," and what I called a false tooth. I quickly learned that I could manipulate the plate with my tongue so that, extended, the one tooth was outside my mouth; and when retracted, I appeared to be snaggle-toothed. Over the years I had lots of fun clowning around with it.

Several years later we moved to Gaines County, Texas, twenty-five miles northeast of Hobbs, New Mexico. Hobbs had a nice night club where we met friends for cocktails and dinner every week or two; and since Joyce liked to dance, we usually made a few turns around the floor. I wasn't very good at it, but I could hold Joyce while she danced. To me, dancing had always meant holding your partner in your arms, which I thought was the best part; however, in the early 1970s, some idiot started a new dance, in which your partner flounced around half-way across the floor from you. I had refused to try it, until one night, after several drinks, I was "feeling like a man oughta' feel the year round." The band was pouring it on, and the floor was crowded with people jumping around, doing the Watusie or "what-ever-they-called-it."

I said, "Joyce, let's dance. I can do that!"

We hit the floor like Fred Astaire and Ginger Rogers. We were dancing ten feet apart; the music was fast, and after a few minutes of burning and turning, I was out of breath and panting like a lizard on a hot rock. All of a sudden—Bam! I blew my false tooth out onto the dark dance floor. I panicked!

I yelled, "Joyce, I've lost my tooth!" as I opened my mouth and pointed.

I had played too many tricks with the tooth, so all she did was laugh and keep dancing. I dropped to my knees and frantically started feeling around on the floor with my hands. The music was loud, so no one heard me as I screamed, several times, "You son-of-a-bitch, get your foot off my hand." Joyce was half-way across the floor, still dancing, and hadn't missed me. A cocktail waitress came over and asked, "Sir, are you having a seizure?"

"Hell no! I lost my damn tooth!"

She brought a flashlight, and together, we searched in vain for the tooth. (Later, I wondered what she would have done if she had found it.) Finally, in desperation, I went to the bandleader, and yelled (loud enough to be heard above the music), "Feller, you're gonna' have to stop this damn music."

He looked me over and mouthed, "Why?"

"Because you've already played "Jeremiah Was A Bullfrog" twenty-seven times, and I can't find my tooth!" pointing to the gap between my front teeth.

He stopped the music and turned on the lights. By that time Joyce had joined in the search, but she was little help because about all she could do was laugh. It was like an Easter egg hunt, with every drunk in the place joining in the search; but I was the one who found it. It was under the foot of J.M. Trent, a car dealer from Denver City, Texas. The Club exploded with laughter when I walked over to the microphone and flashed a smile which showed the gaping hole between my front teeth. I held up my plate in one hand and the tooth in the other and said, "J.M., you son-of-a-bitch, look what you did to my tooth!"

For a long time afterwards, sometimes when I'd meet a stranger on the street, he'd say, "Hey, aren't you the guy who lost his tooth on the dance floor?"

How embarrassing!

CHAPTER 49

Crepes Suzette

As my wife Joyce and I drove into our home town, I looked proudly at the sign proclaiming "Higginbotham, Texas." As self-appointed Mayor and President of the Chamber of Commerce, I had badgered the State Highway Department for years until they finally put up a sign for the city. It was the only town sign I ever saw that said "ENTERING" and "LEAVING" on the same post. The population was thirteen; and when the census taker came by the last time and asked what language was spoken, all but two of us said, "Spanish."

Home had never looked much better, and we were in high spirits as we unloaded the old blue Buick. It was spring time in 1978, and we had just returned from a two week visit with our daughter Danna and her family in New Orleans. It had been our first trip to the "Big Easy" and we had a great time with our family.

Joyce and I had been broke and heavily in debt for many years. We had recently paid off our last note at the bank, so we felt like we had just gotten out of jail. After fourteen years, we now had a little money that we could call our own. We started our shopping spree in Shreveport, Louisiana, at the Libby Glass Factory, where Joyce loaded the car with cases of glassware.

In New Orleans, she purchased gifts, clothes, and enough azalea plants to cover three acres. There were many things to see and do in that historic city—the views of the mile-wide Mississippi River, a ride on a stern wheeler, tours of the battlefields, above-ground-cemeteries, antebellum homes, and the beautiful azalea trails. We did it all. We also learned that creole food is the best in the world;

so we ate, and ate, and ate! We had raw oysters on the half shell, crawfish, shrimp, etouffee, beignets and cafe au lait, strawberry crepes, and my favorite dessert: crepes suzette.

I made a few buys, myself: a T-shirt with an irreverent message printed on it and a book entitled "New Orleans Cooking," which I referred to as my coon-ass cookbook. Transplanted Louisianans are called "Coonies," and the native born are known as "Coon-asses," hence, my name for the book. Louisiana folk counter by saying, "The difference between a coon-ass and a horse's-ass is the Sabine River."

I bought several bottles of various liqueurs and cognac for cooking crepes. The most important purchase was a special pan for making crepes. The pan is about nine inches in diameter with a round bottom. The bottom of the heated pan is dipped in batter, turned upside down, and cooked over the burner of a stove: producing an eight-inch, very thin, pancake-like delicacy. Any kind of food can be wrapped in crepes. They are to Louisiana what tortillas are to Mexico.

I had practiced making crepes while at Danna's house, and decided suzettes would be my speciality. The sauce is made with butter, sugar, and two kinds of orange flavored liqueur. Crepes are folded and heated in this wonderful sauce, then flamed with cognac. It is the "Queen" of crepe desserts. I planned to impress my friends with my culinary art by making this dessert for them.

Before leaving New Orleans, I filled two ice chests with oysters, crawfish, and shrimp. I had so much seafood that cats would surround my car when I stopped for ice on the way home. When we got the glasses, plants, seafood, luggage, and all the other stuff loaded in the car, the back-end sagged like a bootlegger's automobile. As we drove toward home, we planned the "Mother of All Seafood Dinners" for our friends, which, of course, would include my special dessert.

Party night came, and I was dressed for the occasion. I had on my sacrilegious black T-Shirt inscribed: "Jesus Is Coming, And He's Really Pissed," so Joyce was praying fervently that lightning would not strike the house. Each time the door bell rang, she peeped out the window to be sure it wasn't our preacher. I also wore a black beret, which I had bought directly off the head of a Mexican waiter in a joint in Juarez, Mexico a few years before, and I was puffing cigarettes from a long-stemmed holder. It was my picture of a real French Chef.

Five couples came, and it was quite a party. After cocktails, we started with plump oysters on the half shell with plenty of seafood sauce. Some of the guests declined, being unable to bring themselves to eat a raw oyster, but the rest of us agreed they were out of this world. Next came boiled crawfish, boiled shrimp, fried shrimp, and fried oysters. Vegetables were small red potatoes, carrots, and corn on the cob, boiled together with crab boil for an extra spicy flavor. The meal was fit for a king.

Now for the grand finale! The guests were crowded around the table, eagerly awaiting the culmination of this culinary masterpiece, of which I had made such a big production. I had prepared the crepes in advance; so after the table was cleared, I rolled my equipment into the dining room and began to cook the magical sauce. When it was ready, I carefully placed the folded crepes in the pan, and tenderly spooned the sauce over the top. Everything was ready.

Unfortunately, trouble was about to rear its ugly head. No one noticed that I had been sampling the cognac since 5:00 o'clock in the afternoon. It was to be used for flaming the crepes suzette, but I had used quite a bit of it for a different purpose. An alcoholic fuzz had begun to grow in my brain as I placed the hot pan in the center of the table. I had doubled the recipe for the dessert, but when I poured the cognac in a pan to heat, I had mis-measured and quadrupled it. When it started boiling, I quickly poured it over the crepes. The drums rolled, and I struck the match! WHOOSH!! Instead of low, soft blue flames, these flames were going two feet high! All hell broke loose! Everyone at the table was kicking his chair over backward to get away from the fire. I heard someone yell, "You crazy sonofabitch!," and in the excitement one timid soul bolted for the door.

Through the haze in my mind, I realized what was happening. I grabbed the handle of the flaming pan and headed for the kitchen sink, accidentally passing it under a roll of paper towels, which caught fire. I hurriedly filled the pan with water, ruining my wonderful crepes suzette, while Joyce and a couple of guests beat the fire out in the paper towels. All this happened in a lot less time than it takes to tell, but the party was over. The look on Joyce's face told our friends it was time to go home. She was as mad as a wet hen.

When the door slammed shut as the last of our friends departed, Joyce read the riot act to me. We were fifteen miles from the nearest fire truck, and I could have easily burned the house down. She was most emphatic when she said, "You can either quit drinking or quit cooking crepes suzette!"

I still have the recipe, the liqueurs and the crepe pan, but during the last twenty-two years, there has never been another crepe cooked in our house.

Chapter 50

Elderberry Episode

What's purple, has a tart taste and is about the size of a B-B? An elderberry. They grow wild in the Sacramento Mountains of New Mexico.

One weekend my wife Joyce and I were at our place in Cloudcroft, which is in the Sacramento mountains, and we found some of those berries. Joyce said, "These would make wonderful jelly," so we picked a big sack of them and took them back to our West Texas home.

Joyce left on an overnight trip before she had time to make the jelly. The dust hadn't settled on the road behind her when I came up with other plans for the berries.

I had heard about elderberry wine and how good it was, so I got a couple of gallon jugs and started my first wine making project. I didn't know one thing about it, so I made the mistake of asking some of my friends for advice. I got more information than I wanted or needed.

I mashed up the elderberries and put them into the jugs, added some water, a little yeast and sugar; and the wine making process was on. Someone had told me to put balloons over the necks of the jugs to keep air away from the juice, which I did, securing them both with rubber bands. I didn't realize what was about to happen. Nobody had told me to wait awhile to put the balloons on because when the fermentation begins, that stuff gets wild for the first couple of days. I had started the wine early one morning, and when I came in from work that night, one of the balloons was leaking a little around the neck. The other one, however, was about three feet long and tight as a fiddle string. I saw immediately that it was going to have to have some relief or something bad was going to happen. I also noticed the balloon had an awful lot of froth and bubbles in it, and a little of the wine had overflowed into it. I thought I was being very careful as I loosened the rubber band to relieve some of the pressure, but all of a sudden the balloon blew loose. It flittered and danced up to the ceiling of the kitchen—pfloof—pfloof—all over the ceiling. I jumped on a chair, then to the table, and then to the cabinet top, trying to catch that damn thing, but to no avail.

I knew Joyce was due home the next day; and I remembered that once before, while she was gone, I drank a little more than I needed and cooked something that blew all over the ceiling. She was just a wee bit upset while cleaning and scrubbing up the mess I had made. Remembering this, I looked and almost yelled out loud, "Godamighty, there's wine all over the ceiling!" I decided I'd better start scrubbing.

Did you ever try to wash purple wine and pulp off a textured ceiling? It ain't easy!! By the time the next year rolled around, I had bought a book titled "How To Make Wine," quite a bit of equipment, and increased my production to twelve gallons. Against the advice of the book and various acquaintances, I cooked the juice out of the grapes. That was not the thing to do. The wine wouldn't clarify; so I did some wild and strange things, trying to get the sediment out of it. Finally, it looked pretty good, but it was not the best product I ever tasted. In fact, it was bad! Years later, I was discussing the art of fine wine making with a friend, when he pulled a bottle of my wine out of his filing cabinet. I held it up to the light and saw immediately that wine was not the only thing living in the bottle. Something awfully bad was growing inside it, and I didn't think it was a Genie! I hastily made him promise he would never open that bottle, because something really bad might happen to him.

Since I had increased my production, I decided my winery needed a name. In spite of the fact that we lived on the flat, high plains of West Texas, the "Happy Valley Winery" seemed a good choice to me. It sounded sort of like the Napa Valley. I elected myself president and had business cards printed. This quickly became a family project. One daughter, Debby, had some labels made for the bottles. They read, "Dan Fields Happy Valley Winery, Higginbotham, Texas. We will serve no wine before its time." The bottom of the label boasted "OUR FEET ARE CLEAN." Danna, our other daughter, had some bags printed "Just a little cheer from Dan Fields." I bottled that year's crush without too many problems, so I thought I had everything going pretty well.

The next year, I decided to expand my little in-house winery again, and increased production from twelve to forty gallons. Heretofore, I had thought my wife Joyce had a wonderful sense of humor, but I could tell it was deteriorating. I was pouring, pumping, siphoning, racking, and fooling with wine half the time. It was a big job. Joyce was getting fractious and beginning to raise hell about having so much wine in the house. She was also making some threats about what she might do with it. We were still getting along reasonably well until one day she announced, "Guess what: Mother is coming tomorrow! I want to know what you are going to do with all that wine!"

Bottle of Dan's very famous Happy Valley Elderberry Wine. "Our Feet Are Clean"

I replied, "That's a very good question." Joyce's mother is the sweetest lady in the world and a wonderful person, but she is also a very strict teetotaler. The mere mention of the word beer or wine would just set her off into orbit. We could not have her finding all eight of those jugs, so I said, "Well, it's too cold to put it out in the barn. I am not sure the alcohol content is high enough yet to keep it from freezing. So, I tell you what I'm gonna' do! I'm just going to cover it up."

I moved all of it into one bedroom, got a bunch of sheets, draped them over the jugs and prayed some. However, there was no way to disguise the musty aroma which permeated the air. Edith surely smelled it, and after we left for work, I felt sure that she had to have investigated, peeping under those sheets to see what in the world was in that room with the door closed. I guess she was afraid to ask what was going on, because she never mentioned it. That batch of Red Zinfandel and Seville Blanc turned out pretty good.

Christmas came; and guess what gift my friends and family received (all but Joyce's mother)—wine, bread and cheese! I wondered how many friendships would survive the test. It worked out O.K. with the men, but a couple of the wives were upset with me for a while. One of their husbands drank the whole bottle, got completely out of his head and puked all over the house. The other one drank half a bottle of the Red Zinfandel and poured the rest on the living room carpet. It seemed though, that the animosity toward me subsided when I explained to them that the same thing had happened to Ernest & Julio Gallo on several occasions.

Through the years, I hosted several annual "wine tasting" events. Some were pretty lively! Before my last party, I received the following letter from one of my very best friends, Jack.

Mr. Dan Fields
dba Blame It On Dan
Re: RSVP-Homemade Wine Tasting 93

Dear Dan,

As always, Dan, I am thrilled to have received your annual invite to sample your creative endeavor. The sheer genius in how you handle the grapes, the flame, and Joyce all at the same time have certainly been a wonder to all of us for a number of years.

Unfortunately, Dan, I must report I will be unable to join in the festivities this year as Loreen did in fact enlighten me on the aftermath of last year's celebrated tasting event. Loreen tells me that after arriving home last year via our garage wall, I crawled out of the car into our den, and after the smoke cleared she clearly witnessed me wearing what appeared to be a smoked salmon on my toupee. She further claimed that I proceeded to the telephone where I called and challenged my mother-in-law to a yodeling contest. To make matters worse, I apparently won.

I assured Loreen that I had not only absorbed some of the methods of fine wine making but learned a fine culinary talent as well. That's what did it, I'm afraid to say, Dan. As I was trying to demonstrate the art of smoking salmon over a medium gas flame, somehow or other my toupee landed in her waterless cookware and clouded the kitchen with smoke. I'm afraid matters still worsened. You see, Dan, when I grabbed for the fire extinguisher, in my exuberance, I failed to remember that the "Fruits" of our prior years tasting celebration were still in-part hidden in the extinguisher. Well, that's when Loreen really "hit the roof."

Dan, I'm sure gonna miss the fun. Maybe Loreen will cool off by next year.

Your old buddy,

Jack

For a while mine was one of the most famous wineries in Texas; but fame dies, and the Happy Valley label sank into semi oblivion. I've still got some of it left—not much, but a little. Quite often, I bump into old friends and the question is asked, "When are you going to crank up the old 'Happy Valley'?"

My answer is always the same. "Quien Sabe."

CHAPTER 51

Making New Friends

A gentle breeze stirred the tall pines as I was taking my usual walk around the mountain one morning in Cloudcroft, New Mexico, where we had a summer place. It was a beautiful day. The sun was shining; the flowers were blooming, and the birds were singing. It was a fine day to be alive. What a perfect day!!

As I rounded a bend in the road, I met my friend John, who was walking with a stranger. We stopped to pass the time of day, and John introduced me to his friend. It became obvious in a few moments that the stranger was rude. I'm not fond of rude people, so the hair on the back of my neck began to stand up just a bit.

He quickly said, "Fields, that name sounds familiar. What are you famous for?"

I retorted, "Breaking and entering!" in a gruff voice.

He stammered, "Do you make wine?"

"Yes, as a matter of fact, I do," I answered.

"Oh, that's where I've heard of you. I drank some of your wine at a friend's house. How much yeast do you put in your wine?"

I replied, "Three fourths of a teaspoon in five gallons."

He said, "Oh, you put more than that."

I raised my voice a little and said, "Hell, no, I don't put more than that."

He said, "I put a teaspoon in a gallon."

I answered, "I don't give a damn how much you put in a gallon of wine! You asked me how much I put in mine, and I told you."

The conversation went downhill from there. I finally walked away, hotter than a two dollar pistol. He probably could have criticized my wife and kids without upsetting me, but to tell the president of the Happy Valley Winery how to make wine—Hell, no!!

As I walked on around the mountain, back to our place, I noticed the birds were singing off key, the flowers had lost some of their luster, and the damn wind was blowing a gale. It had turned into a sorry day.

I walked into our house, kicking a few things around and muttering, "Crazy son-of-a-bitch" under my breath. My wife, who was lying on the couch, reading a book, asked, "What's your problem?"

I answered, "Well, I ran into this damned old fool down the road—" and started to tell her about my experience, when all of a sudden, she came off the couch about two feet straight up, still in a horizontal position, and yelled, "Of all the childish things you have done during our forty some odd years of marriage, this is absolutely the most childish one that I've ever experienced; you standing out in the middle of the road, arguing with a total stranger over how much yeast you put in a gallon of wine."

What could I say, with snuff running out of both corners of my mouth?

Chapter 52

Wrong Number

There is a description of a fisherman which says: "Behold the Fisherman. He goeth forth early in the morning filled with hope. He returneth when the hour is late, smelling of strong drink; and the truth is not in him."

This is a fish story. It is not about the big fish that got away. It is a true story about the time the fishermen got away.

Howard, a lifelong friend of mine, invited me to come to Colorado City for a different kind of fishing. He said, "Dan, if you will get one of your friends with a fast boat to come with you, we'll catch more fish than you would believe. I have a dandy telephone, and we'll "call up" some catfish."

The telephone he was talking about was taken from one of the old phones that you cranked to make it ring. It was a generator with two wires attached. When the wires were thrown into the water and the phone was cranked, it set up an electrical field which would temporarily stun large catfish. Howard and I had used one on previous occasions with amazing results. It was better than a boat load of fishing tackle. I should also add that it was highly illegal to have a phone in your possession anywhere near a river or lake.

Lake Colorado City was built by Texas Electric Company to provide water to cool the generators of a power plant and Colorado City was allowed to use the water for municipal purposes. Texas Electric maintained control of the lower half of the lake to secure the dam, generating plant and hot water discharge. They fenced it and hired the Pinkerton Detective Agency to patrol both the land and lower lake. The upper lake was open to the public for recreational purposes while buoys with appropriate signs divided the two areas.

A neighbor of mine, Jess, owned a boat that fit Howard's description. He was probably the most nervous person I had ever known. The slightest bit of excitement would cause him to go into a tizzy. He was definitely not the kind of person you would prefer to take on this kind of trip; but he had the boat and would have to do, so I invited him, with considerable apprehension. Jess was elated when he was invited. He had never done this kind of fishing and was as excited as a child.

When we arrived at Howard's place on the prearranged Saturday morning, he had been busy getting ready for the day. He had lined up two more guys to go with us. One of them was his cousin Don, who had been a classmate of ours and was almost as jumpy as Jess. The other fellow was an old, tongue-tied, exbootlegger named Jack. We needed two boats, so Jack provided the second one. Needless to say, he was a funny, funny man.

Howard had learned that the Lake Patrol boat was out of commission, so all we had to look out for were game wardens (or so we thought). If a game warden approached us, we would drop the phone in the lake.

We finally got organized about noon and set out down the lake. Howard, Jess, and Don in the lead boat with Jack and me bringing up the rear. We had all agreed to go up a certain narrow creek to do our "calling." The water was deep and calm, an excellent place for large catfish. We drove past the buoys as if we owned the lake, waving at the people at the power plant as we passed by. We were in the middle of the lake when the motor on our boat began to cut out. It would run for a while and then almost quit. This caused us to fall a long way behind. We lost sight of the other boat as they entered the creek, while we struggled along with the troublesome motor.

Suddenly, a serious problem developed. From our location I could see a Lake Patrol pickup drive up on the hill beyond the creek.

I couldn't see Jess's boat, but I watched as the patrolman got out of the pickup.

I said, "Jack, those boys are going to get caught."

He had not seen what was happening until then. Meanwhile, I started circling out in the middle of the lake to see what was going to happen.

Jack yelled, "Dat ton of a bitch is tootin' at dem boys!"

I asked, "How do you know? You can't hear above the sound of our motor."

He answered, "I taw the moke from dat gun!"

My reply was, "If there's any 'tootin' going on, our guys won't be there very long. I don't think Jess can stand the smell of gunpowder."

We continued to circle for an interminable time, while a number of shots were fired. I began to wonder if someone had been hit. Three minutes passed.

All at once, here came Jess's boat around that point! We were a half mile away, but I was sure that I could see Jess's hair standing on end, and maybe Don's as well. I'll bet there wasn't four inches of that boat touching the water, it was going so fast. They drove straight across the lake and I couldn't believe my eyes! They threw out the telephone lines again!

I said, "Jack, we might as well get out of here. That's Howard's idea to keep fishing, and there's no way that Jess is going to stay down here. I know him."

We limped along until we were approaching the buoys which marked the restricted area, where, our friends passed us. They were going so fast that we thought we had stopped.

The City Lake Patrolman was sitting in his boat at the buoys watching the activity; however, he couldn't have cared less about what we were up to. We stopped to say, "hello." I'm sure he knew what was going on; but with a grin, he asked, "What are you boys doing?"

Jack replied, "We were donna do tum fitchin, but dis ole motor wouldn't run."

The patrolman said, "There damn sure wasn't anything wrong with the motor on the boat that was with you."

We headed up the lake and didn't go far until we met Jess and Howard. They had carried Don to a friend's cabin, left him to hide the phone, and came back to see about us.

Jess was white as a sheet; so unstrung that I thought he might jump out of the boat. Howard was laughing so hard he could hardly tell us what had happened.

He related this story: When they stopped up the creek, they were unaware of approaching trouble. They had thrown out the phone lines and started cranking when the patrolman called out, "You are trespassing, and I am ordering you to come to shore."

Howard had yelled back, "Go to hell!"

To Jess and Don he hollered, "Boys, let's get out of here!"

Jess was turning flips and grinding on the starter at the same time. The motor would not start!

When they refused to come ashore, the Patrolman fired several shots into the water near the boat. After the first shot was fired, Don was lying in the back of the boat, rolled up in a little ball, screaming, "If you don't get this SOB started, I'm gonna' swim for it!"

They finally realized that Don had kicked the gas line loose. They quickly plugged it in; the motor started, and they were on their way.

After a lot of laughing and screaming, we went to the cabin where Don was pacing the bank. He was as shaky as Jess.

I said, "Don, Howard said you were a little nervous during the excitement back there."

He replied, "I wasn't a damn bit scareder than that SOB you brought from Gaines County. He was leaping from the front of the boat to the back, yelling, "This damn thing has never failed to start!!"

For weeks afterward, I sometimes woke up from a deep sleep, laughing about the fishing trip.

Chapter 53

Pompano en Papillote

Several years ago Joyce was away from home one weekend on one of her many Eastern Star sojourns, and our son David had come by to spend a weekend with me. He was driving an eighteen wheeler loaded with pipe, headed for Farmington, New Mexico. He planned to leave late Sunday afternoon and drive into Farmington during the wee hours of Monday morning.

We had a nice weekend. We were sitting around Sunday morning, drinking coffee and shooting the bull, while I leafed through my coon-ass cookbook. I found a recipe which certainly looked interesting, and I mentioned it to David. It was called Pompano en Papillote, meaning fish in a bag, a specialty of Antoine's, a famous New Orleans restaurant. The fancy dish is made with many ingredients and cooked in parchment paper shaped to resemble a balloon. After we discussed it for a while, we agreed that Joyce would come in that afternoon worn out from her trip and certainly not in the mood for company for supper; but the more we talked about the special dish, the more intriguing it became.

I finally said, "David, I've seen your Mom mad plenty of times, so one more won't make a hell of a lot of difference. Let's go to town, buy the ingredients for this recipe, and invite Kelleys out for dinner tonight. Mary Nell can give me some advice; Kelly can mix the drinks, and we'll have dinner ready when your Mom gets home."

David and I went to Hobbs, New Mexico and bought the works for the gourmet meal.

The recipe called for butter, flour, onions, parsley, white wine, salt, white pepper, red pepper, heavy cream, shrimp, crab meat, oysters and pompano. We could not find parchment paper, so we decided to use some paper bags to cook the wonderful dish in.

We decided we needed a vegetable dish to go with the fish, so we found another delightful recipe in the book called Brabant Potatoes. The potatoes are diced, fried at a fairly low temperature, removed from the fat, and fried again at a higher temperature. Finally, they're covered with a wonderful garlic butter sauce.

We called the Kelleys, invited them, and they were pleased to be involved in testing such a special, unique dish. We told them to come early so we could prepare everything and have dinner ready by the time Joyce came home.

They came out about 4:00 o'clock that afternoon, and we sat down to have a drink. Before we finished our drink, I looked out the door and hollered, "Godamighty, there's Joyce, She wasn't due for two more hours!" She didn't look too pleased when she came in and saw that we had company. However, she is a good sport; and I'm sure she decided she might as well make the best of it.

I thought I could cook all that food in a few minutes, with very little help, but things didn't work out that way. Soon I had everyone in the house peeling, chopping, or stirring. It was a hell of a job!

David had planned to pull out for Farmington pretty early, but things got so interesting he couldn't bring himself to leave until he saw how the meal turned out.

It turned out great, maybe some of the best food I have ever eaten; and everyone else, even Joyce, agreed that it was worth all the trouble it had been to prepare it.

The Kelleys went home; David headed for Farmington; and Joyce and I went to bed. We were asleep in three minutes.

About 3:00 o'clock in the morning, I woke up and yelled, "What in the hell is that ungodly odor in this bedroom?" I realized that it was Joyce's breath from all the garlic on the potatoes. When she heard the racket and roused up, I said, "For God's sake don't breathe out the window, your breath will set the shinnery south of the house on fire."

It was several days before we could get near each other because of the garlic on our breath.

Chapter 54

Leroy

One afternoon while I was working at South Plains Industrial Supply in Lubbock, Texas, I stopped to say "hello" to an old black friend of mine whom I had known for many years. He was visiting at the front of the store with the boys on the parts counter. Leroy had worked for a gin machinery company for a long time, but had been retired for a few months.

He was always happy, jolly and smiling; a most likable fellow. He was also an ornery rascal before he retired. He did his part to liven up East Lubbock on weekends. He would start drinking at 5:00 o'clock on Friday afternoon and start tapering off about five minutes until 8:00 o'clock on Monday morning. He had obviously slowed down some since his retirement.

He was riding a bicycle that day, and I asked, "Leroy, why are you riding that bicycle?"

He replied, "Oh, Mr. Dan, I can't afford a car. Since I retired, I jus' don't have the money to drive one."

"Do you have any money?"

"Mr. Dan, I haven't got a nickel."

"I don't want to see my friends out of money." As I said that, I pulled out some money, gave it to him; and he went on his way.

A couple of months later, he came by the office and handed me several small bills. It was the same amount I had given him.

I asked, "What's this for?

He answered, "That's what I owe you."

"You don't owe me any money, Leroy. I gave you that money, I didn't loan it to you. It's yours."

"No, I'm not gonna' have it."

"Yes sir, you are, too."

"No, I may need some more sometime."

"O.K." I said and stuck the money in my pocket.

That happened from time to time through the years; but sometimes when I asked how he was doing, he would reply, "I'm doin' fine, Mr. Dan, jus' fine." That meant he had some money.

I remember once he came by, and I said, "Leroy, have you had a beer today?"

"Oh, no, Mr. Dan, I quit drinking."

"Quit drinking! Why did you do that?"

"Well, sir, I can't afford it. I just get $137.00 a month from social security. You can't drink no beer on that kind a' money and eat, too. I had to quit."

When he was broke, I gave him a little money; but he always brought it back, with the same explanation, "I want to pay you back. I may need some more sometime."

One day he came by, and the smile wasn't there.

He explained, "They condemned the old house where I live, and I'm gonna' have to move. I don't know what I'm gonna' do. I just pay $50.00 a month for it, and it's an awful old shack; but it's all I got and I can't afford anything better. I just don't know where I'm gonna' live!"

I felt so sorry for him; however, I later found out that he was allowed to stay in the old house.

One day, after I had given him some more money, he said, "Oh boy, now I can get me some wine and lottery tickets."

I said," I don't care what you do with the money, Leroy, it's yours, but I thought you quit drinking."

"Oh, no sir, Mr. Dan, I couldn't do that; ain't no way. I couldn't live like that."

Another day he came back into my office with a smile on his face like a wave on a slop bucket. His eyes were sparkling!

I asked, "How are you doing, Leroy?"

He said excitedly, "Guess what, Mr. Dan! I won $1700.00 last night shootin' dice. Come out here and let me show you somethin'."

I went to the door and saw an old car he had bought. I was so proud for him. He was just beaming. He gave me some money, which I didn't count at the time. I stuck it in my pocket, but later when I looked at the money; I was sure it was more than I had given him. Maybe that was his way of paying interest. I was so happy for him and glad to see him doing better.

I saw him once after that. He was still driving the old car, still smiling, eyes still bright.

I asked him once more, "How are you doing, Leroy?"

He said, "I'm doin' fine, Mr. Dan, I'm doin' jus' fine!"

Chapter 55

The Empty Grave

"Yep, they buried him alive," I heard Pop say. He was talking about Byrd Jackson Cochrain, a colorful character who had lived in West Texas around the turn of the century. I was about seven years old and I was fascinated by the tales I had heard about Cochrain.

About seventy years later, I decided to pursue my interest in his eventful life. One day, I drove to Stonewall County, Texas, which had been his old stompin' grounds. My nephew, Raford Hargrove, and I went to see Byrd's grandson, Steve, and his wife Eileen. We spent a delightful afternoon at their home with them, Byrd's daughter, Juanita Powers, and her daughter, Pam, sharing memories of Byrd.

The following episodes from Cochrain's life are from what his family told me and what I had learned from my folks.

My grandfather, W.C. Davidson, owned a hotel at Clairemont, Kent County, Texas from about 1902 until 1910. My parents, Julius Lundy Fields and Frances Rebecca Davidson, were married there in 1909. Since Kent County borders Stonewall County on the west side, my folks knew many of the stories regarding Byrd Cochrain and the people in Stonewall County.

Byrd's grandfather, Henry Byrd Cochrain, came from Ireland—washing dishes on the ship for passage to America—and landed in New York. He later went to Sedalia, Missouri, where he married Hannah B. Houston, who was born in Caddo, Oklahoma and was Sam Houston's niece. They moved by wagon to Montague County, Texas, and he died there many years later. Hannah eventually moved to Seminole, Texas, where she died.

Stephen Byrd was the youngest son of Hannah and Henry Byrd Cochrain. He married Maggie Crowell Perry and upon her death married Cordelia Louisa McGuire. Byrd (B.J.) Jackson was their oldest son, born in 1883 in a dugout in Wilbarger County. He was one 1 of 11 children. Byrd had about a sixth grade education taught by his father. Times were really hard and he hated farm work anyway, so at 12 years of age he left home to try cowboying to make a little money in order to help the family. His dad told Byrd that when things got better he wanted him to come back home and finish his education, but he never did. He gave Byrd a good horse and headed him out to look for a job on the DDD Waggoner Ranch, south of Vernon. Dan Waggoner hired him and paid him $15.00 a month and beans. This is still the largest ranch in the United States: 500,000 acres under one fence.

Byrd became friends with the Indians who had helped him find the Waggoner ranch. He enjoyed horse racing with them and you could often see him racing across the prairie with an Indian girl behind him, her arms around him.

While he was working for the Waggoner Ranch, he sent nearly all of his money to his folks, so he didn't have decent clothes, just cast offs, and the other cowboys made fun of him, calling him a kid and a nester. One man called Red, took up for him and they became friends. Years later, after they had both quit the ranch, Byrd was out near Portales, New Mexico, and saw a man lying on the ground. He had been shot, and was near death. Byrd picked him up to take him into Portales to the doctor and realized it was Red, his old friend from Waggoner Ranch.

Meanwhile, times continued to be hard for the Cochrains, with years of very low rainfall and little grass. There was no more money coming in since Byrd had quit the ranch because he was unhappy with the fact that the herds of smaller operators were drawn into the large herds as they were driven through the country and very little effort was made to separate them.

He later owned a race horse and made money running him

and riding bad horses, betting on his ability to ride them, while continuing to send money home. At first his mother refused to use the money because she knew it was made by gambling, but was eventually forced to use it to survive. His mother was a strong willed woman and had to be tough to survive the hard, lonely life she lived. She loved to talk and would take her children on one horse with her to ride five or six miles to see a neighbor. This was true of so many women living in West Texas at this time, because there were so few people to visit with.

He and his mother didn't get along very well and even after he was grown and had children of his own, when she came to visit sometimes she would say, "I'm just going to give you a whippin'." He would back up to her and say, "Whip away!"

Juanita said, "Grandma was exceptionally clean, keeping the sand in her yard swept to the hard ground around the little three room house where she lived. When Grandma came to see us, she nearly killed my brother Pete and me for the first few weeks after she got there, having us pull broom weeds out of the yard and sweeping it clean. Daddy kept his stuff on our little screened back porch and she would say, 'You've got a shop, the bunk house and I don't know how many barns. You don't need to put this stuff on the porch!' So he reluctantly moved it all off, then as soon as grandma left, Daddy started bringing all those oil cans and stuff back to the porch. She was about 86 years old at this time and she rode a horse side saddle when she came to visit us. When she went under a clothesline or low hanging limb, she would lean backward instead of leaning forward which scared everybody to death. It could easily have caught her under the chin and killed her."

The last time she came was in 1950 and Steve remembered she was really spry and still rode a horse, but shortly after that, she fell and broke her hip. They discovered that she had never been in a hospital before, but they found that she had scars from broken ribs and such from the past. She never recovered from the broken hip and was buried on New Year's day.

When Byrd was about sixteen he went to work for the Diamond A Ranch in southern Arizona. During this time he and eight other cowboys decided to go into Mexico and steal gold from the Yaqui Indians. The Indians ambushed them and killed all of them except Byrd and one other man. Juanita said she guessed he got in trouble everywhere he went! Once he remarked, "God takes care of me. One time I was about to be ambushed by a group of men. A terrible storm was coming up and suddenly a streak of lightning, like a wall of fire, struck between us and while they were blinded, I turned and got away."

Byrd returned home from Arizona because his dad needed some help but did not stay there very long. Later, he and his father went to Seminole, Texas where each of them bought four sections of land in Gaines County. His father looked after both places while Byrd went to Midland and South Dakota for a while to work.

Another story of Byrd's younger days took place near Midland, Texas. While he was working for the Half Ranch, an old cowboy that he worked with was always getting drunk and falling off his horse. One night Byrd was coming home to the ranch and found the old drunk passed out on the ground with his horse standing by him. Byrd killed the horse, took out his insides and sewed up the drunk inside the horse's belly with only his head sticking out the rear end of the horse and went on to the ranch.

The next morning some children were walking to school and saw a bunch of hogs gathered around a horse lying on the ground. They thought the horse was yelling, "Sooey, Sooey!" It scared them, so they ran back to their house and screamed, "Mr. Smith's horse is laying up by the gate hollering 'Sooey' to the hogs!" When the parents came down to investigate, they found the man in a very embarrassing position. He told them that the coyotes came in the night and tried to eat him, but were easily scared off. However, the hogs came when it got light and they were another matter. He thought they were going to eat him alive. Byrd never tired of telling the story of the little white headed children yelling, "His horse is laying up there talking to the hogs!" As long as he was in that country he said he never knew of the old cowboy taking another drink.

Mr. Half sent a train load of cattle from Midland to the Dakotas and had Byrd and another young man go with them. The night after they loaded the cattle at Midland and were waiting for the train to leave, they were watching black couples come out of a church by the tracks. They were "loved up" as they walked to a nearby well for a drink of water. The well was surrounded by a wooden box. Byrd and his friend decided to move the box a few feet beyond the well while no one was watching. When the next couple came out to smooch a little and have a drink of water, they fell into the open well. Byrd and his friend heard someone yell, "Some so-and-so done went and move this here well!" About that time the train whistle blew, they jumped on and left Midland in a hurry.

They unloaded the cattle somewhere in the Dakotas and drove them to the ranch. A violent thunderstorm came up and they got wet and nearly froze. Byrd said the lightning was so intense, that fire was jumping between the horns of the Longhorn cattle. Few people have seen that phenomena. They also saw the northern lights while up there, another awesome sight.

This reminded me of a story my Dad used to tell about gathering wild Longhorn cattle out of brushy country. They would drive them out of the brush, but could not keep them out. They finally started roping the cattle as they drove them out of the brush and twisted wire as tight as a fiddle string between their horns. After a couple of days of the cattle banging their heads around in the brush, their heads got so sore, they would not get close to any kind of brush, so they were able to drive them where ever they needed them to go.

Juanita said, "Daddy told us that while they were in South Dakota, flour was so scarce, they ate potatoes in the place of bread."

She added, "Daddy also used to tell us funny stories about when he was out in the Dakotas. He and another cowboy were gathering wood, killed a bear and found that she had two cubs; one male and one female. They caught them, named them Jack and Jill, tied them in the back of the wagon, and started back to the ranch. Jill fell out of the wagon and hanged herself, but they made a pet out of Jack. Every time anybody went to town they bought candy and let Jack find it in their pockets. A city slicker came out one day, saw the bear and decided he wanted him. He was smoking a cigar while he had the bear sitting on his shoulder. He blew the smoke in the bear's face and the bear boxed him good. He yelled, 'Keep your danged old bear! I wouldn't have him!' "

When Byrd returned to Texas from the Dakotas in 1912 he went to Bradshaw to buy some cattle for his ranch in Wilbarger County. While he was there he met Ethel Hancock. He spent the night there and told her he'd be back in two weeks to get her for his wife. He did just that. She was his first wife (except for the Indian girl he had for a while.) He was married several times and had nine children from two of the wives. Juanita Powers was next to the youngest of the second family.

Byrd claimed to have been a Texas Ranger and worked for a Captain Russell at one time, but Juanita visited the Ranger Museum in Waco and the only Russell she found record of was too far back for the right time period. She now wonders if he actually was a Texas Ranger. She remembered her family talking about a lot of cattle rustling going on around Graham and at that time Byrd was working for the Cattlemen's Association. Byrd told her that Captain Russell asked him if he would consider going to Magdelena in Socorro County, New Mexico as an undercover agent for the Cattleman's Association, because some of the cattle stolen in West Texas were showing up there. Russell also thought that the climate might improve Ethel's health; she had been sick since she started having children in 1913. Byrd decided this was an opportunity he should not pass up, so he moved his wife and four children to Magdelena, where he bought a small ranch in about 1917. Moving that far was an enormous project, but Byrd thought Ethel would love New Mexico. Unfortunately, she hated it, worrying constantly about the dangers of his job.

He soon discovered that the stolen cattle were indeed being moved into the country and that Sheriff Baca was involved with the rustlers. He also suspected a gang by the name of Cooper was involved in the thievery.

Early one morning a neighbor, (a widow lady), rode over to his place and said that Clay Cooper and his three boys had stolen her milk cow. Byrd and a neighbor went to Cooper's Ranch and saw that they had just finished skinning the cow. A shoot-out ensued and Clay and one of the boys were killed. Since Sheriff Baca was involved with the Coopers, he helped capture Byrd and locked him in a tool shed. They planned to hang him later that day. While they were eating, a little Mexican girl unlocked the door and let Byrd out. Her name was Juanita and Byrd's daughter Juanita Powers is named after her. He escaped, but was later recaptured, put in jail, and charged with the murder of the two Coopers. His friends made bond and he was released, so he and his wife Ethel (who was pregnant again at that time), and their four boys headed back to Texas in covered wagons.

Sheriff Baca, upon hearing that Cochrain was leaving the county, gathered a posse and caught him just outside Socorro, New Mexico. Byrd told the sheriff in no uncertain terms that he was not about to go back to Magdalena until he was able to deliver his pregnant wife back to Wilbarger County, Tx. Baca insisted, but when Ethel poked a double barreled shotgun out from under a tarp covering the wagon, Baca decided that it would be in his own best interests to let Byrd go, and returned to Magdalena. Cochrain was out on bail, so he knew that after he delivered Ethel and the boys home to Texas, he would have to come back to Magdalena to stand trial for murder.

Juanita said, "Many years later, my cousin's husband was working on the highway near Magdelena as an engineer. My cousin said as the family traveled through the lava beds west of Carrizozo, she wondered how in the world her grandparents could possibly have traveled through that rough country with two wagons and their children."

Once when Byrd was passing through southeast New Mexico, he ran into an old friend, Tom Ross, a thief he had known since his days at the Waggoner Ranch. Tom was stealing cattle all over that part of the country and urged Byrd to "throw in with him" but Byrd refused. He had never stolen anything. He had learned his lesson at an early age when he and a group of cowboys went into Mexico to try to take gold from the Indians.

Several years later, two Cattlemen's Association men were after Ross and his partner, Milt Goode, for stealing cattle and planned to present their case to the Gaines County, Texas grand jury the next day. They were spending the night in Seminole, Texas, at the Pittman Hotel, when Ross and Goode burst into the lobby and murdered them both. The outlaws escaped, but they were finally caught and sent to the penitentiary. Later Ross escaped from the pen and fled to Wyoming, living there until his death.

I told Juanita and Steve that my parents knew Tom Ross' reputation and said he was one of the toughest outlaws in West Texas. He was known far and wide as one mean hombre.

When I was a young man, I moved west to a community twenty-five miles northeast of Hobbs, New Mexico. Ross' home ranch had been located between our ranch and Hobbs and I passed by it many times, curious because of all the stories my folks had told me about him.

In 1918, when Byrd got back to his ranch in Wilbarger County, Texas, he loaded his three freight wagons with all their worldly goods and moved his family to Stonewall County. The Pruitt brothers owned a ranch there, which they sold to Cochrain, so they could return to their previous home in Gaines County, Texas.

A month or two before he was supposed to return to New Mexico for trial, where he knew he would be killed, he took out an insurance policy so that he might leave some money for the family. Ethel was opposed to him buying the policy, so he didn't tell her he had bought it.

During this time there was a flu epidemic going through the country. In February of 1919, Byrd and Ethel both came down with it. He was still sick in March, unable to return to New Mexico. Several people were dying, so Byrd and some of Ethel's cousins, the Hoggets and the Archers, came up with the idea of having him "die," thus releasing the friends in New Mexico from their bonds and saving Byrd's life. When Ethel was told about the plan to have Byrd "die," she cried and begged Cochrain not to do it.

The Emspanger family, who owned the White Ranch, were also in on the deception. Mrs. Emspanger was a nurse and knew how to draw blood, so she drew enough blood from Cochrain to make him look pale.

Friends spread word that Cochrain was sinking fast and they called for the doctor to come to the ranch. He finally came and confirmed that Byrd was indeed very ill. Hearing Byrd was sick, "Uncle" Pat Anderson went out to the Cochrain place to see him. He was one of Byrd's best friends but did not know about the deception because he was as honest as the day is long and would not have allowed it. When he got there, Byrd was laid out on the kitchen table with coins on his eyelids and they told Pat he had died. As he returned to Aspermont, he met the doctor and told him of Byrd's death. The roads were muddy and bad, so the doctor turned around and went back to town. He wrote out the death certificate, and sent a copy to the sheriff in Magdalena, New Mexico telling him they need not expect him to return to New Mexico for trial. The doctor would not have taken anyone else's word regarding Byrd's death, except "Uncle" Pat's, saying, "If Pat says he's dead, he's dead." Neighbors even came by to pay their respects and view the body. One of his close friends later swore that Byrd winked at him as he viewed the body but he didn't tell anyone about it for a long time.

When they faked Byrd's death, they actually had graveside services and prepared to bury him in the pasture south of his house on a little hill. Joe Jones, a favorite of Byrd's was his pallbearer twice, when they staged his death in 1919, and again 60 years later when Byrd actually died. That fact came out in the *Ft. Worth Star Telegram*.

After throwing a few shovels full of dirt on the casket, Mr. Hogget and Mr. Archer and another friend told everyone to go on home because it was raining and cold; that they would finish covering the grave. After everyone left, they let Byrd out of the coffin. He told them that when the dirt started hitting his coffin, he really wanted out of there! Together, they filled the grave, then Byrd got on a horse and headed south.

Later, Hogget and Archer went to the penitentiary for helping Byrd fake his own death. The third friend left the country and avoided prosecution.

Eventually, the insurance company paid off the policy, thinking Byrd was dead. Ethel was pregnant at this time and had TB. After the baby Pat was born (the only one of their children born in the green house in Stonewall Co.), Byrd moved the family to a ranch north of Sterling City, Texas. They had lived there about two years when someone told Byrd that stories were going around back home that he was not dead. The insurance company and sheriff were planning to go to the grand jury with charges of fraud. Byrd figured his time as a free man was running out.

Ethel was so sick they were forced to move into the old Landmark Hotel in Sterling City, where she died. Pat was about two years old and Jesse was eight. Jesse said he barely remembered his mother's death. Byrd's sister, who lived in either New Mexico or Arizona, heard of Ethel's death. Believing Byrd was dead, she was concerned about the 5 little boys Ethel had left (Jess, Sam, Earl, Russell and Pat.) She called the sheriff in Sterling City, (Sterling County, Texas) for information about who had the children.

He said, "Their Daddy is taking care of them."

She replied,"Their Dad was my brother and he has been dead for two years."

"No, he's very much alive!" said the sheriff.

After some investigating, he realized that this man was the Byrd Jackson Cochrain, who was supposed to be dead. He called the Sheriff of Stonewall County, and together they went out and dug up the casket. It was empty. From that day on, Byrd was known as "Deadman Cochran"

They kept Byrd's tombstone at the green house in Stonewall County. At one time, a group of colored cotton pickers were living there, and they were fascinated by it, but when Juanita's brother Pete told them the casket was in the attic, they all left that night, under cover of darkness!

Cochrain was arrested and charged with defrauding the insurance company, but was later released on bond. He moved the five boys back to the green house in Stonewall Co. and Aunt Mattie came and cared for them. Grandma and Grandpa Hancock, Ethel's parents also came and helped. Then he met Bessie Boyston. She was taking care of her blind father and her mother who had lost her mind. She needed some help with them and he needed help with five young boys, so they married. Bessie and Byrd eventually had four children; 3 girls and a boy. Juanita Powers was next to the youngest.

Byrd J. Cochran kneeling beside his own tombstone in Stonewall County.
(Courtesy of Stonewall County Historical Society)

Byrd was soon tried and sentenced to two years in the penitentiary, but served only a little over a year. While he was in the pen the warden had the prisoners making whiskey from the corn grown on prison land and was making a ton of money selling it. While they were chopping cotton one day along the Brazos River, Byrd was helping an older, sick prisoner keep his row up. The farm boss struck Byrd across the back with a bull whip and told him to hoe his own row and let the other man hoe his. The older man fainted and the farm boss sat there on his horse and cut him to bits with the bull whip. After the guard beat the old man to death, he forced Byrd and another prisoner to throw his body into the Brazos River.

When he got out of the pen, he changed the spelling of his name from Cochrain to Cochran, to save embarrassment to his family. He had lost his ranches in Sterling and Stonewall Counties and still owed his bondsmen in New Mexico, so he started making whiskey, a trade he had learned while in prison. He bought back his Stonewall County place; first buying 320 acres. He bought another quarter section every time he got enough money. Because of his nickname "Deadman Cochrain," a sharp bend in the road near his house is still known as "Deadman's Corner." He also paid off the bondsmen in New Mexico.

Stonewall County Sheriff Bailey Bingham came out and told Byrd they were going to revoke his parole and send him back to the pen for making whiskey. They gave him a few days to get his business in order and he served about another year.

The very first morning after he was released from prison, he told his boys that he had dreamed there was water in the old hand dug well at the house. When they went down in the well and started digging, they found whiskey that he had hidden there before he went to the pen so he didn't have to kill any time getting his whiskey business started again. However, he had also hidden some down in Coon Hollow by a creek below the house, which they never found.

Years later, a close friend, we called "Uncle" Sid, moved to Rule and came out to pick cotton for Sam. Sam was Byrd's son and Steve's dad. Sid had heard about the whiskey so when it was too wet to pick cotton, he would walk up and down the creek, poking a wagon rod in the ground, looking for the hidden whiskey, which he never found. Sid told Steve he really wanted to find that whiskey because he had always wanted to drink some that was as old as he was.

Steve said. "Granddad Byrd may have just told him that it was hidden there to give him something to do."

Steve said he didn't know who was the toughest, his dad Sam or his granddad Byrd as evidenced by the following stories:

Once Byrd had a fight with a Mexican and the Mexican hit him in the head with a blunt ended ax. The doctor put a metal plate in his head with no hair covering it. Later he was digging a well, walling it up with rock. His son Sam and grandson Steve were up on top, sending the rock down to him. A 2" x 6" board slipped from the top, fell into the well, hit Byrd on the head and knocked the plate out. It was about 4:00 o'clock in the afternoon and he went ahead and finished his job in the well with blood streaming from his head before he came out.

The subject of how they got wells symmetrical when they dug them so deep by hand came up. Steve said they laid a big metal wagon tire on the ground and as they dug out from inside it, it dropped down, keeping the walls straight.

As Steve had said, his dad Sam was tough, too. When he was about 60 years old, he was out on one of the ranches, working on a windmill when the top rung broke and he fell 30 feet to the ground. The fall broke his hip but he drug himself to his pickup, pulling up grass along the way to help propel himself. He said he passed out two or three times along the way. He finally pulled himself up to get into the pickup, fell over into it and passed out again. He had previously fixed a rope on the gate to make it easier for the girls to open. He thought at first he would drive over the gate, but decided he might ruin his radiator so that he would never get to town. He finally drove up beside the gate, cut the rope with his pocket knife, the gate fell down, and he drove over it. He got to a neighbor's house and she called an ambulance. When he regained consciousness at the hospital, he immediately told somebody to go fix that gate so the cattle wouldn't get out.

Juanita said, "Of all the many tragedies in our lives, one that my dad never got over was when two of my brothers, Earl and Pat turned an old stripped down car over. It threw Earl out and the fender was resting on his neck. His little brother Pat was trying to lift the car off of him, when a neighbor, Loss Smith passed by and didn't even stop. When Loss got to town and told somebody about the wreck, they hurried out to check on it and found Earl was dead. Byrd always hated Loss for that."

Byrd had a grocery store in 1927 west of Aspermont where they lived when Juanita was born. He had an old stripped down truck and he would put Juanita, as a baby, on a pillow in the truck when he went to Stamford for supplies. Juanita's mother stayed to tend to the store. Owning the grocery store was a good excuse for buying lots of sugar which he needed for his whiskey operation; and the boxes that inner tubes came in were just the right size for transporting quart jars of whiskey.

Uncle Jesse told Juanita that one time someone sent word to Byrd that the Revenuers were coming to his place the next day. He and John Duncan, who was working for him, buried all the 30 gallon kegs in a nearby field and then plowed all night with teams to cover any tracks of where they had hidden the whiskey.

Steve and Juanita mentioned that at one time people grew quite a bit of cotton in that area, along with the corn for whiskey. I told them that I remembered my parents telling me about cotton being grown in the Clairemont area.

I told the group as we visited that I remembered when I was 5 years old, I had heard that the sheriff at Snyder had confiscated a still. Dad and I were in town and I begged him all afternoon to take me to the jail to see it. I could imagine it was some huge, frightening piece of machinery, but when we got there, all I saw was a bunch of old rusty barrels and some copper tubing.

Byrd was very particular and always used copper boilers for making his whiskey. Some of his neighbors didn't have copper boilers and used barrels. Byrd told Juanita that people were taking their lives in their own hands if they drank much whiskey made in barrels. That's what caused a crippling disease known as Jake leg. I mentioned that I remembered a lot of Jake legged people.

Juanita said, "Dad, Uncle Boss Edwards and Uncle Mark Duncan argued all the time about who could make the best whiskey. Dad grew his own corn and used lots of yeast, malt, sugar and water. People who were not so particular colored their whiskey by throwing a sack of Bull Durham tobacco into it, but my daddy went to Eastern Oklahoma and brought back hickory logs, chipped them up and baked them until they were a golden brown, then used them to color the whiskey. His whiskey was clear as water until he put the chips in to color it."

Some of Byrd's best business was around Old Glory, which was a German community about 17 miles east of their house. He liked the people down there. The community was originally named New Brandenburg and during World War I, the folks there were flying the German flag. A bunch of the local people went down there and tore the German flag down, put up the American flag and renamed the town Old Glory.

Juanita said everyone around there made whiskey, but her dad and Dan Hill's brother, Roy Hill, were the only people to go to the penitentiary for it. Dan had been working at his still about twenty miles north of Deadman's Corner and heard that the Revenuers were coming so he left. Roy rode up to the still just as the Revenuers arrived, so they thought he owned the still and arrested him which caused hard feelings among their families.

Juanita had married by this time and she told me, "My in-laws, the Powers, lived north of town and were also making whiskey."

I said, "Everybody in Stonewall County must have worn armbands to keep from selling whiskey to each other!"

She laughed and said, "Early in the mornings, from our house you could see the smoke from seven fires where neighbors were making whiskey. Some of those were Uncle Boss Edwards, Dad, Dan Hill, Ropers, Thunderburgs, and Bakers. Rutherfords and Smiths operations were south of Aspermont but Sam Tanner, the biggest boot-legger in the whole country lived to the southeast. He was making lots of money selling whiskey while his neighbors in Stonewall County were just making enough money to buy groceries."

He was the only bootlegger anyone knew of that put his whiskey in bottles, instead of Mason fruit jars, and put his own private label on them. He had copied the picture of the dark haired lady from the Baker's Best Hair Tonic bottles for his label and called his whiskey "Tanner's Best." He hauled most of what he made to Fort Worth and Dallas, Texas. It is said that his whiskey was served in the finest bars in those cities. Some people thought he worked for the Chicago Mob.

The question arose: "Did Sam Tanner have an operation on Rough Creek?" No one seemed to know for sure, but my brother-in-law Tom Hargrove told me many times, that he remembered seeing Sam's truck everyday, loaded with whiskey, passing their place west of Rotan.

Sam's wife and two daughters lived in Ft. Worth, most likely to keep them out of harms way. There were two accounts of Sam's death. Steve Cochran thought Sam's assailant shot him off a tractor and threw him in the hog pen to be eaten by the hogs at his place southeast of Deadman's Corner.

Upon hearing that story, Juanita Powers exclaimed, "Well, it's just like a lot of the other accounts, somebody always makes a good story out of it! However, I have always heard that Sam was messing around with one of his truck driver's wives and the driver found out about it. The driver came in one afternoon while Sam was in the pen feeding his hogs, jerked an old 30-30 Winchester out of his truck and blew a hole in Sam the size of a Number 3 tomato can. The hogs, smelling blood, promptly ate Sam's body, leaving only his skull and a few of the larger bones. I think the man who shot him lived across the river from my folks.

I told them, "I have heard that the day before Sam's murder case went to the grand jury, the only witness to Sam's killing was killed in an accident on a horse. He had tried to jump a good fence right by a gate; the horse failed to clear the fence, fell on him and killed him. He knew enough about horses that he would not have tried to jump the fence unless he was in a terrible hurry, otherwise he would have opened the gate and walked his horse through."

Was someone shooting at him? That question will never be answered.

Juanita said, "Things went on in Stonewall County that didn't happen anywhere else in the world." What an understatement!

The friendship between the Cochrans and the Tanners was strong and Sam Tanner's land has been under lease to some of the Cochran family for more than 50 years.

The colorful, adventurous life of Byrd Jackson Cochrain began on October 5th, 1883. He "died" on March 10, 1919. The colorful, adventurous life of Byrd "Deadman" Cochran began on October 5th, 1883 and he died in 1970. He was 87 years old.

Chapter 56

Hot Stop

My mother's brother, Carol Davidson, was my favorite uncle. When he was a young man, he was small in stature; and as he grew older, he became more and more frail. He might have weighed 115 pounds if he had been soaking wet. He wasn't much bigger than a "washing of soap."

He married his last wife when he was in his eighties. She was a big, fat woman. Uncle Carol was as cold natured as anyone I ever knew, and she was the exact opposite.

They had an old DeSoto automobile; and when they traveled, she drove. The old car had an air conditioner that could freeze water on the front seat. His wife turned the air conditioner as high as it would go, and Uncle Carol nearly froze to death. He finally learned to take his overcoat and two or three quilts, get into the back seat and wrap up with just his nose sticking out.

One afternoon in August, they stopped for gas in Cisco, Texas. The thermometer registered 108 degrees; not a leaf was moving on the trees in that part of the country. It was hot! Uncle Carol came digging his way out from under all those quilts and, still wearing his overcoat, stepped out onto the driveway of the service station. He had turned a little blue from the cold; he was such a frail, little old fellow. He was stooped; and with his hands clasped in front of him, shaking and shivering, he turned to the service station attendant and in a quivering voice, asked, "Is there anyplace around here where a man can get warm?"

The attendant took two steps backward, looked at him in disbelief, and said, "My God, man, just stand there a little while!"

Chapter 57

Mama

What can I say about Mama; there are so many things. She was one of eight children born to William Maxwell and Mary Ellen Davidson. She was named Frances Rebecca, but was known as Fannie all her life. She was born in Erath County, Texas on March 23, 1890. When she was eleven years old, she and her family went to Elida, New Mexico in a covered wagon to visit relatives. Once, she showed me where they camped for a night at the foot of the Caprock, west of Gail, Texas. That night the work horses got away and went back toward home. Her brother's saddle horse had been hobbled, so he was still there; and as soon as they missed the other horses, he rode back to look for them. The family was forced to camp there for an extra two or three days, waiting for her brother to return with the teams.

When they finally got to the top of the Caprock, she told me they saw only two ranch houses between there and Elida, New Mexico. On the return trip, her folks found some land they could buy in Scurry County, Texas, southwest of Snyder. They bought 800 acres for $1100.00 and moved to Scurry County that year. Her brothers grubbed the mesquite off the land and put it into cultivation. The weather was dry and they made very little crop for two years; but her father was a good trader, dealing in horses and cattle, so they got by. Mama had finished the sixth grade in school before that trip to New Mexico, but never returned to school. However, she had a good self-education.

A couple of years later, they moved to Clairemont, Texas and opened a hotel and livery stable. My grandfather also had a contract

Frances Rebecca (Fannie) and Julius Lundy Fields.

to deliver the mail and, occasionally, carried passengers from Clairemont to the Double Mountain Fork of the Brazos River, north of Rotan, Texas.

My dad, Julius Lundy Fields, was cowboying in the area at that time, and ate at the hotel frequently. That is where he met my mother, and they were married there on May 9, 1909.

I remember how Mama's eyes twinkled and she laughed as she told a story about Dad and eight black prisoners. They had been locked up in a little red rock jail for quite a while, for shooting dice. Mama's folks had a contract with the county to feed prisoners, and they were losing money on that deal. They sent Dad to the jail with an evening meal; and the next morning, the jail house door was open, and the prisoners were gone. Mama used to laugh and say, "Julius turned them out, didn't you?" He never answered, but just grinned.

He did say, "I don't know where they went, but they had a heck-uv-a-long walk in any direction from Clairemont!"

My folks had five children, the first of which died in infancy. My mother never talked about the baby, but I know it was on her mind an awful lot. I was the youngest of four children, born in 1926. Mama

Jail at Clairmont, Texas.

was thirty-six years old when I was born, and the other children were nine, ten, and twelve, so I got more attention than I deserved. She had the most wonderful wit and sense of humor. These are the traits that I remember most about her.

When I was five years old and started to school, she told the teacher, "If my son misbehaves, just whip the boy next to him; and it will put the fear of God in Dan."

Most all she knew was hard work and hard times. I can remember when she washed clothes in a No. 3 tub and wrung them by hand; and how happy she was when Dad brought in an old Maytag washing machine with a wringer. She still had to heat the water in a cast-iron wash pot and rinse the clothes in a No. 3 tub, but that was so much easier than doing them on a rub board. She ironed them with a "sad" iron, heated on the wood stove in the kitchen. In addition to that, she made clothes and patched them for all of us. She always let me pedal the old Singer sewing machine, which I loved to do. I could pedal it a "mile a minute." She kept house and cooked three meals a day for a family of six. My sister Bargy helped her when she was not in school; but most of the work fell on Mama's shoulders. We always grew a garden and killed our own beef and hogs, and Mama canned all of it. During the depression, that was how she fed the family. She worked all the time but always took time to spend with me if I needed her.

Suppertime around our house was one of the best times. It was always a fun time of the day, with everyone sharing their experiences. I'm sure the conversation was pretty much the same every day: what happened at school, whose team of mules ran away, how many tubs of clothes Mama had washed, or which one of the neighbors had stopped by that day. That's where Mama's love of life, wit and sense of humor showed up.

She and I were the only ones in the family who could carry a tune, and some of my favorite memories were of when she and I would sing the old Methodist hymns together. Our favorites were "Amazing Grace" and "The Old Rugged Cross." When we wanted to jazz it up a little bit, we sang "Give Me That Old-time Religion." We probably knew every song in the old Methodist hymnal, and I still remember many of them. These were wonderful times for me as a child, and though we were poor, I didn't realize it. She taught me to read by reading the labels on cans and flour sacks. She also taught me that anything I did should be done well.

Mama's social life consisted of church and an occasional game of dominoes with our neighbors. Sundays were special, and our house was a favorite gathering place for neighbors and their families. After lunch, there was lots of visiting and games for the kids.

What little she had, she shared with others. If a neighbor was ill she was the first one there with food and comfort. In 1919 there was no crop and no money at all; and when Christmas came around, there was not a grain of sugar in the house. She traded the watch my father had given her for two pounds of sugar so the family might have some sweets for Christmas.

There were very few arguments around our house, because Mama would say, "Get out of here if you want to fuss!" I am sure her she and Dad disagreed occasionally, but not around us children.

She never wished for a better life, but was content with the one she had. She lived in a shack with no indoor plumbing until she was 60 years old, and was most appreciative when she was able to move into a nice house.

Since we lived near her for many years, Mama's favorite pastime was spoiling our children; and the kids adored her. She told wonderful stories to them, and her memory was as sharp as her wit.

In 1952, my folks moved to Higginbotham, Gaines County, Texas, and Mama was in her glory when she and Dad bought the first TV in the community, because they had a house full of company every night. Mama enjoyed the visiting more than the television. She saw the good in everyone and was certainly not a gossip, but didn't mind accidentally hearing a little of it.

We always had a dog around the place that stayed outside, and Mama had a kind of "don't care attitude" about the dog. Once when she and Dad were visiting my brother J.C. in California, he had a small house dog which Mama certainly did not approve of. One night she put her dentures under the bed and during the night the dog chewed up her false teeth. I think she finally forgave J.C., but never forgave the dog. From that day forward she hated every dog that ever lived. Years later, J.C. came to Texas for a visit and noted that a dog had made a mess on her front lawn. When he mentioned it, she said, "I'm going to take care of him right away!"

J. C. asked, "How do you plan to do that?"

She explained, "I'll stir up some grease, cement, sugar and just a little bit of cheese. That will fix him for good!"

Occasionally, Mama would decide that Dad was getting a little too heavy so she always threatened him with a diet of a lettuce leaf and a black eyed pea.

My folks never drank nor condoned it; but when Dad was in his seventies, he had some heart problems. The doctor prescribed three tablespoons of whiskey a day. He usually bought it at Dan's Bar, which was near where we lived. He always paid cash; but once he bought a pint and realized he had left his billfold at home, so he gave them a check. He never made that mistake again! When he told

Mama what he had done, she chewed his ass out until it wouldn't hold shucks. She asked, "What will Red and Stuffy (our bankers) think? I'm sure she thought they looked at every check that came through the bank. From then on when Dad started to Dan's Bar, he made sure he had plenty of money.

My folks moved to Snyder in 1966, and Dad died the following year. Mama lived alone for the next six years. Once during that time, she fell, hit her head and woke up lying in a pool of blood. My brother Rex, who lived in Snyder, rushed her to the hospital, then called me and told me what had happened.

He said, "Mama was 'knocked a little silly' by the blow and has decided she's going to die."

I said, "Godamighty, as strong willed as she is, if she thinks she's going to die, she will."

I took off to Snyder; and when I got there, she was still off center just a little bit and laughing.

I asked her, "What's so funny?"

She answered, "I don't think Dr. Pierce is coming back to see me."

"Why?" I asked.

She explained, "I chewed him out good for cussing."

I assured her he would be back the next morning, and sure enough, he was. Her mind had cleared by then, and she told me she had apologized to him.

She said. "I told him I was sorry, and that I had a few fences of my own that needed mending."

All of us, including the doctor, thought this was pretty funny, since she was a devout Christian and a lifelong Methodist.

When she went home from the hospital, Rex and our sister Bargy hired a lady, Mrs. Jones, to take care of her and help around the house. Two weeks later, Mama fired her. Rex phoned me and told me what she had done. I went down to help out and stopped at Rex's business before I went to her house.

He said, "Don't mention Mrs. Jones to Mama. We were at Bargy's house the other night and her name came up, and Mama went into a tirade. She literally had a fit and used words I never dreamed she knew, so we don't bring Mrs. Jones name up any more."

I laughed, because the worst word I had ever heard her say was "shoot."

Rex and Bargy came to Mama's house for dinner that night, and we had a good visit. After they went home, Mama and I talked for a while. Suddenly her jaw set in a way that I had seen before. It always meant that she was about to get down to business.

She asked, "Did they tell you about the fit I pulled the other night?"

I answered, "Yes Mama, they told me."

"What did they say about it?" she asked.

I said, "They told me you just raised hell!"

She said, "Good, I just wanted to be sure they told it right. I was sick and tired of that old lady. She was all sweetness and sugar when some of you were around, but she was mean to me when we were alone. I finally got fed up with it and ran her off. Rex and Bargy kept talking about what I had done, so I finally got enough and put a stop to it."

I said, "Mama, I can see their point of view; they're the ones who have to find someone else to stay with you." I hesitated for a moment, then added, "But I don't blame you a bit; I would have done the same thing."

You should have seen the smile on her face!

In 1973 her health deteriorated. She had been sick with stomach trouble all of her life, using a stomach pump every night for more than fifty years; but I never heard her complain. Now, at eighty-three, she was diagnosed with a hiatal hernia. She decided to have surgery to correct the problem, but never recovered.

I was with her at the end, sitting by her bed at the hospital. She had been uncomfortable and hurting some, and then she just suddenly drifted away. I thought she had gone to sleep until a nurse came and told me she was gone. She had gone away as she had lived, quietly, in her own gentle way. It was hard to believe for a moment, but I was not as heartbroken as I could have been, because she had lived a long and happy life, and had imparted much more happiness than she had received. She probably lived in the years of the world's greatest change, from riding in a covered wagon to seeing a man on the moon.

She had lived the life she wanted to live, seen most of her grandchildren, and suffered no more pain. Dad had been gone for six years, and much of the sparkle that had always been in her eyes had not been there since then.

I know most people think their mother was the best one ever, but I know for sure mine was.

We buried her beside Pop at Camp Springs, Texas, where I was born.

A great lady was gone.

Chapter 58

Father's Day

Today is Father's Day. As I sit quietly in our den, my thoughts go back in time to the memory of my own father. He was forty years old when I was born, and I was the youngest of four children.

As a child I followed him while he worked from daylight 'til dark. His patience, strength and love spread over me like a warm blanket. I was never able to talk much to Dad, but I always knew, without a doubt, that he loved me. I guess we both thought a show of affection might be a sign of weakness. However, when I needed a hug and an outward show of love, my mother happily provided it.

Although he had very little schooling, Dad had learned all he needed to know to provide for our family. He was as smart as a whip. He was a good farmer, an excellent cowman, and could make a work mule or a saddle horse climb a tree.

He neither drank, smoked nor cussed, but said little of those who did. He had a sense of humor, and enjoyed a good joke, although I never heard him tell one.

As I grew, Dad taught me how to straddle a horse, how to rope a steer, and to hit the first lick in a fist fight; however, he was not much help when it came to driving either a car or a tractor. He started too late in life to be good at either one; once I saw him drive a tractor through two fences, while hollering "Whoa," as though to stop a team of mules.

He also taught me that if you danced, you paid the fiddler; but when I got in a bind (and there were many times), he was always there to help.

I was gone from home for a few years during World War II, and it was not an easy time for either of us. Pop was sixty-years-old and working way too hard in his farming and ranching operations; so in 1947, urged by my brothers and sister, he offered me a partnership in his business. I was married by then and working for Continental Oil Company, looking for oil with a seismograph crew. Dad's offer was too good to pass up, so I jumped at the chance. Many father-son joint ventures don't work, but ours did.

Through the years, we were involved in a number of different enterprises. We ran combines and built terraces for the public. We also traded cattle in addition to our bread and butter business, which was farming and ranching. We seldom disagreed, although each of us had a mind of his own. The only time I refused to help him start a new project was when he wanted to put in a dairy, which I knew to be a full time job. When Dad mentioned it to me, my response was, "Hell No! If you want a dairy, you'd better get someone else to help you with it!"

"Why?" he asked.

"I'll tell you why. The only thing that keeps me from having a steady job on this outfit is about six hours a day—from 10:00 o'clock at night until 4:00 o'clock in the morning when I can sleep a little. I don't need another job!"

"Well, that's fine, if you aren't interested. I just thought it might be a good opportunity."

I didn't think so at the time, but he had a good idea. It would have been a very profitable business for us.

Dad was a quiet man, but when his piercing blue eyes peered under dark, bushy eyebrows, everyone knew he meant what he said. I never saw anybody mess with Dad. He was as tough as an old boot on the outside, but gentle and tenderhearted within. He was a strong man mentally and physically, who quickly knew the right side of any issue that arose, and had no patience with anyone who chose the other. Fiercely independent, he taught his children and grandchildren to think for themselves.

As the years passed, Dad seemed to depend on me more and give me most of the responsibilty in our operations. He prepared me for the time when we could no longer make joint decisions. I grew older and thought I understood Pop a little better. His mother had died when he was a baby, so he missed out on childhood because of a mean and abusive stepmother. Maybe that was the reason he loved our family so intensely. When Dad was thirteen, he and an older sister Ella, moved out of their home near Rosebud, Texas and lived together in another house on the family property. At age fourteen, he took off alone for the coal mines at Thurber, Texas. Around 1903 he went to Clairemont, Texas, where he worked as a cowboy on several of the ranches in that area. That is where he and my mother Frances Rebecca Davidson, were married, in 1909.

They moved to Scurry County, where I was born in 1926; then in 1939, we moved to Mitchell County, where Dad and I later began our partnership. In 1952, we all moved to northwestern Gaines County, where we ranched and farmed adjacent to the New Mexico State Line.

Dad hung up his plow and put his saddle in the tack house for the last time when he was eighty years old; then he and Mom left Gaines County and moved to Snyder, Texas. It was quite a change; we had lived near each other for a long time. Dad and I had been together almost every day for twenty years, and I missed him.

As Father's Day of 1966, approached, I sat down and wrote the only letter I had ever written to my father. I told him he was the best man I had ever known. I thanked him for the sacrifices that he and Mom had made for our family, but mostly I thanked him for the many things he had taught me: integrity, honor, generosity, kindness and love. I also thanked him for teaching me the value of hard work, that a handshake meant more than any contract, to pay my debts, and to look folks in the eye when I talked to them. I didn't say "I love you," but he knew I did.

The letter was never mentioned; but when I saw him a few days later, the look on his face told me that he had read it. I was so glad I had written to him, because by the next Father's Day, he was gone.

Chapter 59

The Latter Years

On June 30, 1989 at the age of 62, I retired from State Line Coop Gin at Higginbotham, Texas. Joyce and I had discussed where we might go to spend our remaining years.

She said, "Kerrville, in the Hill country of Texas, is a beautiful place."

I replied, "We don't know a damned soul in Kerrville, and we have a lot of friends in Lubbock, so let's move there." Joyce agreed.

Dan and Joyce in their new Lubbock, Texas home.

Ten days after we moved, she said, "Dan, the last few days, I've had twice the husband and half the money I've been used to, so you'd better get the hell out of this house and find a job."

While I was president of the Plains Cooperative Managers Association, I helped organize South Plains Industrial Supply—a Cooperative Cotton Gin machinery and parts business located in Lubbock, and served as Chairman of that Board until I retired in 1989.

The manager of the supply store had mentioned to me that in the three years they had been open they had never had an outside salesman.

He said, "Dan, would you be interested in the job?"

Remembering what Joyce had said, I quickly accepted. I realized that it was a perfect fit. I knew every cotton gin manager in West Texas and they knew me. These were the people I would be calling on. As salaries went, it wasn't much of a job, but it was more fun that any job I every had—visiting my old friends and making new ones!

Nine months later, Joyce and I took a vacation to Florida and the morning I returned to work, the Chairman of the Board met me at the door with a set of keys in his hand.

He said, "Dan, the South Plains Industrial Supply Cooperative manager is no longer here, and guess who the new one is!"

It was not too hard for me to figure out his name was Dan Fields.

I said, "Look, if I had wanted a job with a lot of problems, I would have stayed at the gin where they paid a hell of a lot better than you guys. I'll help you out until you find a permanent manager, but you'd better find one pretty quick!"

I left seven years later!

The job was a killer. The store had a lot of problems, financially and otherwise, and I knew nothing about managing a retail business. I worked day and night and made lots of mistakes, but finally got things turned around and going in the right direction.

We made money every month except for one during the seven years I managed the store.

When I finally got my feet on the ground at the store, I had a little more free time than I did when I was farming, ranching, trucking and managing the gin, so I decided I needed a hobby. Joyce and the kids had begged me to jot down some of my experiences, so I wrote diligently for a while. When I showed it to the kids, they said in unison, "Oh, no, Daddy, we want stories about all the crap!"

I mentioned this to one of my church friends Lea Kidd, and before I knew what was happening, she had loaded me up in her car and took me to a creative writing class which she attended. The class was taught by Nancy Kastman-Scott, a retired writing teacher from Kansas. She was wonderful. She provided me with a world of encouragement and the belief that I might be able to write. For one of my first assignments, she handed me the picture of a baby and said, "Write a story about this."

Now, what in the hell do you write about a baby? I sat for a long time without a clue, but suddenly a funny story came to me. This is what I wrote:

BUBBA, JR.
By Dan Fields

> This here cute, lil' feller is Bubba, Jr. He's shore a chip off the ole block. Brought a lotta pleasure to me an' his mama Judy Jo, too. Lil' Bubba ain't but nine months old and already weighs twenty-six pounds. Fattern' a town dawg. He's shore gonna' be a big 'un when he grows up. He's got the biggest hands and feet and bawls—bawls all the time.
>
> Would you believe that Nancy gave me an "A" for that?

After a while I looked around and every friend I had played golf, so with our son David's encouragement, I took up the game. It was a fun game, but at 63 years of age and not being very well coordinated (I couldn't walk and chew gum at the same time), it was almost impossible to learn. My friends called it golf. I called it knock 'em back. You knock the balls by the hole, then you knock 'em back, and knock 'em back and knock 'em back. I know I started playing too late in life, but I enjoy it. It's a good game: when I tee off, I love watching that hoppy little ball hopping, hopping, hopping along the ground.

What I really enjoy is all the nonsense my friends dish out, and they put up with me, because I throw in a little bull and a few jokes myself. Also, I just hand them my billfold when we start and tell them to take out what I owe when we finish. And . . . I have this bottle in my golf bag. It's a half-pint of blackberry brandy and on rare occasions, when my younger friends wear me out completely, I take a big drink of that brandy to help me finish the game. I carry that particular kind because it tastes so damned bad that I can't drink much of it and my friends won't drink any of it. One day, one of them decided he would try it, but I had to hold a gun to his head to make him swallow it.

Gene Beck was one of my favorite golfing partners and over the years we must have logged a million miles together in a golf cart. He was a good listener so I put the finishing touches on some of my favorite jokes for him. I think his favorite story was about the Duke of Windsor.

It went like this: Several years ago, an ole' West Texas cowboy friend of mine by the name of Coley Johnson raised a colt that was a running booger. Ole' Lightning Bolt won every major meet in the United States and made Coley a lot of money.

Eventually, he was invited to run this horse in a special race in England, so he carried Ole' Lightnin' over for the race. While saddling his horse on the day of the big meet, Coley noticed the Duke of Windsor was in the next stall with his own horse. Coley introduced himself, feeling quite honored to be in the presence of royalty.

A few minutes later, the Duke saw my friend slip a small white pill into the corner of Lightning Bolt's mouth. The Duke became very agitated and said, "Aye say, my good man, I saw ye doping your 'orse. This is highly illegal, and I'm goin' to report ye to the proper authorities."

My friend said, "Aw, Duke, don't get excited. That was just a little ole' sugar pill. The horse likes 'em, and I give him one every now and then. He doesn't like the taste of the bit, and this sweetens up his mouth some. I eat 'em all the time, believe I'll just have one right now. They're mighty tasty, would you like to have one?"

The Duke replied, "Well, old Chap, I don't mind if I do."

Just before they started to parade the horses on the track, Coley called his jockey aside and said, "Son, when the race starts, I want you to take this horse to the outside and keep him there. We don't want anyone to get hurt in this race, because I'm gonna' tell you somethin'. There's only two things at this race track this ole' son-of-a-bitch can't outrun. One is me, and the other is the Duke of Windsor!"

Word soon got around among my friends across the state of Texas that I really loved the game of golf, so in 1990 when the Texas Agricultural Cooperative Council TACC (headquartered in Austin, Texas) decided to hold a managers conference in Ruidoso, New Mexico, Billy Connors, Executive Director, called me and asked me if I would coordinate a golf tournament for this meeting. It became an annual event, and when Tommy Englekey became Executive Director, they continued to ask me to hold the golf tournament.

In the spring of 1997, South Plains Industrial Supply bought Consolidated Bearing and Supply, our principal competitor and I became President of that company. On June 30th I retired from the business but having already planned the July golf tournament for the Ruidoso conference, I went there to take care of what I thought would be the final meeting with my lifelong friends

Was I in for a surprise!! TACC had a reception during the conference each year and at the end of this one, I was called to the podium and presented with several gifts by friends along with a lot of hot air and well wishes.

Then came the grand finale—Master of Ceremonies Jim Taylor

Jim Taylor of Plains Cotton Cooperative Association presents a plaque to Dan which reads "Dan Fields Invitational Golf Tournament."

announced:"Dan, the Council has named the golf tournament we hold each year in your honor and I present this plaque to you which reads "Dan Fields Invitational Golf Tournament." Each year, the winners names will be engraved on this plaque. Now, this means that you will need to come back each year to make the presentations to the winners."

I couldn't keep the tears from my eyes. It was one of the nicest things that ever happened to me.

Several years have passed and the Council still allows me the honor of coordinating the tournament.

As I write this, I am 78 years of age and Gene Beck is still my favorite golf partner. By listening, he has learned a lot about me. He even smiles when I let loose with a string of expletives after missing a putt. He pleased me greatly when he wrote the following poetic tribute to me:

ODE TO DAN FIELDS
By Gene Beck

Let me share a story
About this fellow I know,
A saint, a scholar,
I hardly think so.

A devilish grin,
A twinkle in his eye,
Won the heart of a princess;
God only knows why.

He made her his queen,
This lass from Sweetwater
Blessed him three times:
A son and two daughters.

Farming, ranching,
Driving old trucks,
Whatever it took
To scrape up a buck.

Hauling whatever,
Grain, cotton, baled hay.
Send out the bills,
Not all want to pay.

Park them old trucks,
At least for a time,
Take up a job
Out on the state line.

Ginning king cotton
Most of the time.
Squeezing out grapes,
Making fruit of the vine.

Making his brew,
Wheeling and dealing,
Some come uncorked,
Make a mess on the ceiling.

Retire, move to Lubbock,
Take up the good life,
Can't get much better
For husband and wife.

Cable television,
Pizza brought to the door
No cess pools, no pressure pumps,
Who could want more.

Time on his hands,
Needing spice in his life,
Picks up the reins
At the co-op supply.

Five days of work,
Two days off
Live in the city
Got to play golf.

Callaway, Big Bertha
Golf balls and tees
Run out to the course
With the annual fees.

Team up with a partner
A wager is cooking
Tee up in the fairway
If they aren't looking

Get ready, cart partner
You'll get a full load
Of wisdom and wit
From this king of the road.

"Boy, oh boy," he says,
"That shot was a dandy.
Not quite on the green
But it looks mighty handy!"

Was that a compliment?
I don't think so,
He explained it one time,
This fellow I know

It's your turn old man,
Have you found you a tee?
A beautiful slice
Out into the trees

Over and over
He's faced this same test:
Which club should he use?
Foot wedge is best.

We have quite a time,
This fellow and me.
If BS was music,
A brass band he'd be.

A saint, a scholar,
I hardly think so,
But he's quite a dandy,
This fellow I know.

Glossary

No. 3 washtub — a galvanized tin tub for washing clothes
alley — runway bordered by fences in a stockyard
awful — terrible, terribly
banged around — inflicted punishment
beat the tar out — whipping up on
blazing stump — burning piece of wood
Blue Norther — Blue horizon as Polar Air approaches
booger — scare, scary
broadcast binder — mechanical harvester
bueno — good (Spanish)
built a loop — made a loop in a lariat
bull — male bovine
bullwhip — long braided leather whip
burn shoe leather — to run
burro — donkey or jackass
busted his ass — fell on the seat of his pants
cattle guard — a metal guard, across which cattle would refuse to walk
caught a cattle truck — hitched a ride on a truck for transporting cattle
cheek of the bridle — side of a horses bridle
choused — ran around, pushed cattle
cistern — pen, underground tank for catching rain water
clean their plow — beat up on someone
clods — lumps of earth, clay, etc.
cold jawed — a horse you can't stop
combine (in farming — a mechanical harvester
coming to Jesus — being saved, as a Christian; a serious "this is the bottom line" discussion
contrary — stubborn
corral — a pen (enclosure) for horses, cattle and other animals
cotton allotments — acres allowed to be planted by the government
cows weren't gathered up — running loose in the pasture
cranked up — started up, rared up

crowd-pen — small enclosure for animals
cultivator — machine for loosening the earth
cut him out — separate an animal from the herd
cut loose — releasing
dead run — running as fast as you can
dickering — negotiating
disc — plow for loosening the soil
dither — agitated
dog around — waste time
donkey — ass
double shot — twice the dosage
dugout — hole dug out and covered with sod for living quarters
earthen tanks — hole dug in the earth for catching rain water
feed the bundles into — a combine — pushing bundles into a threshing machine
feeling her oats — feeling good
field day — a good time
filly — young female horse
fixed, fixin' — repaired, on the verge of, preparing
fodder — sorghum for feeing livestock
full tilt — running fast
getting his bluff on — intimidating
got a hump in her back — a horse preparing to pitch
greenhorn — someone ignorant of country life
grilling — questioning
gypsum — chalky rock found in the earth
had the bit in her teeth — a horse running out of control
half hitch — a kind of knot in a rope
harrow, harrowing — a flat device drug on the ground to break up chunks of earth
hemmed her up — ran an animal into a corner
hollered — yelled
hoofing it — walking
hooves — the horny covering on the feet of certain animals
hot under the collar — mad as a hornet, angry
irrigating, irrigation — pumping water from wells to water the crops

jackass vs. mule vs. donkey vs. burro —
jake leg — a crippling condition caused by drinking bad homemade liquor
jillion — more than a million, a lot
keep my nose clean — behave well
kicked the staples out — kicked out the barbed wire retainers
la vida — life (Spanish)
lariat — rope
Long Tom single barreled — name for an extra long single barreled shot
loosened him — came partially separated
lope her out — gallop away
made up a pot — took up money for a bet
mesquite — a tree native of the southwest
messed around — loafed
messed up — made a mistake
mule — hybrid, cross between a horse and an ass
nester — farmer moving into ranch country
odds and ends — miscellaneous
old shotgun — gun
ornery — contrary
pick handle — wooden shaft for a hand tool
picked at — teased
pitch — an animal attempting to dislodge it's rider
plug horse — a worthless horse
posted our land — not allowing trespassers
Quien sabe? — Who knows? (Spanish)
raising sand — having a fit
rare up — raising up on hind legs
rared back in the saddle — riding confidently
rarin' to go — eager
rattle the fence posts — shaking the ground
reins — leather straps for guiding a saddle horse
riding it out — waiting for the end
rigged up — prepared
riggin' — part of the saddle
roan filly — dappled, young female horse

rode off into the sunset — departed, left for somewhere unknown, perhaps never to be seen again

roused up — excited or stirred up

rub board — antique ribbed metal devise for hand washing clothes

ruckus — a violent disagreement

running cattle — ranching

sad iron — one-piece heavy,flat cast-iron with a handle on top — heated on a stove for ironing clothes

saddle horn — the projection on the front of a saddle

salty — tough

sand in our craw — inhaled the sand

sauntered — walked slowly

scraped up — gathered together

seine minnows — net small fish for bait

serape — Spanish shawl to cover the body

set sail — leave hurriedly

shinnery — short oak trees that grow in arid West Texas, derived from French word for oak "chene"

Sí, Señor — Spanish for yes, sir

side saddle — type of saddle for a lady riding with both legs on one side of the horse

slack in the rope — loosen tension in a lariat

snubbing post — a post in the middle of a pen for tying animals

snub-nosed — a short barred pistol

snuff running out of both corners of my mouth —

sow belly — bacon

spinning like the latch on an outhouse door — whirling rapidly

spooky — nervous or scared

steer (vs. bull) — bull that has been castrated

stirrup — foot rest on a saddle

stompin' grounds — where you hang around

sure enough sway-backed, red roan horse's ass — the worst kind of ass

tapping around on — pecking or hitting on something

terraces (on farmland) — large borders for holding rainwater on farmland

thrashed — beat up

thrown their hat under him — joke to scare a horse or cow

tied to a post — tied to post of a fence
tin culvert — a galvanized round pipe for drainage
tolled into the pen — led into a pen by promise of feed
too light in the seat of the pants — too small
took the wheel — started driving
tow-headed — small boy with tousled hair
trap — small enclosure near a barn
tug off a set of harness — large strap which connects a work horse to a plow
turn it on — rush
two teacher school house — a small country school with only two teachers for all grade levels
two-holer outhouse — a privy which will accommodate two people
useless as teats on a boar hog — no good
wall-eyed fit — an uncontrollable tantrum
warm under the collar — see hot under the collar, same but not as mad
watering — person who needs an enema
watering hole (bar) — saloon
wetback — anillegal Mexican immigrant
wetting the hook — fishing
Whirl Away — a famous race horse
Whirlwind — air whirling violently upward in a spiral motion
whose garden needed — someone who needs an enema
wood stove — stove fueled by burning wood
work her over — to beat up on her
worked the kinks out — to work with a horse until it calms down
working the calves — branding, earmarking and vaccinating
wreck, wrecked — thrown from a horse
Yanquí — tribe of Indians living in Mexico
Yearling — a year old animal
yelled — called loudly

INDEX